Hot Springs
and Hot Pools
of the Southwest

JAYSON LOAM

August 28, 1918 - February 22, 1994

In this world when a man dies usually only his immediate family and a few close friends share in the inheritance. As Jayson's son I derive a great satisfaction knowing that, if you are holding this book and reading these words, you too are sharing in that inheritance. Jasyon Loam created Aqua Thermal Access publishing and the *Hot Springs and Hot Pools* guidebooks in order to share with us the simple joy he experienced sitting in the natural warm water of a hot spring alone, or better yet, with a few close friends. The fact that his books exist is a testimonial to his gregarious and generous nature.

Jayson spent the last few years of his life doing what he really loved to do; researching, writing and publishing his books. He spent months on end driving thousands of miles to remote locations, camping out in all kinds of weather. Often underfunded but always undaunted, he pursued his dream with unconflicted desire. I have never seen him happier. My father spent his entire life in search of a truly satisfying outlet for his many talents. He finally found it. Underlying this odyssey was an ever present search for truth in life. Whether he ever discovered the "ultimate" truth I don't know. But he did discover, and more importantly, lived these simple truths:

Be true to yourself.

Do what you truly love to do.

Follow your heart.

His business associate and close friend, Marjorie Young summed up Jayson's passing quite succinctly. "Jayson was an extraordinary presence. There is such a huge absence where he used to be." An absence yes, but not a vacuum. His memory lives on in those of us fortunate enough to know him and be touched by his special presence. And his inheritance lives on every time anyone settles into the enfolding warmth of a hot spring and remembers to think of him and to thank him for helping them get there.

Thanks, Dad. We miss you.

Gary Sohler,
March 5, 1994

Hot Springs and Hot Pools
of the Southwest

Jayson Loam
Marjorie Gersh

AQUA THERMAL ACCESS

Grateful acknowledgments to:

Staff members at state parks, national forests, national parks and hot springs resorts for their cooperation and encouragement; Dancing Man Imagery for Pmts, John Ryan for computer cover design, Jim McEachern for maps updates, and Aptos Post for color separation proofs and negatives; everyone who has ever offered new information about any hot spring and all of the subjects who so graciously consented to be photographed.

Front Cover Left - Deep Creek / 169
Front Cover Right - Glenwood Springs / 46
Back Cover - Pulky's Pool / 130

Photo Credits: Lee Baxandall: 28BL; Dave Bybee: 94L, 132, 137, 138, 143; Marjorie Gersh-Young: 8, 97, 98L, 133BR; Luis Gonzales: 102, 115BL, 117R, 122, 125L, 147; Justine Hill: 27T, 30LB, TR, 31, 75, 77L, 78R, 85, 86, 90, 91, 92; Skip Hill: 27BL; Tim Murray: 54; Gary Sohler: 69; Melanie Sohler: 136; Steve Sutherland: 162; Vic Topmiller: 84; 136; Phil Wilcox: Front Cover Right, 23, 24, 25, 33T, 36R, 38R, 39L, 43R, 47R, 48, 53, 54T, 58, 59T, 65T, 64BL, 101R, 117L 123, 124, 128, 129, 130BL, 131BR, 135T, 140, 141, 182; Rob Williams: Baja section.
Jayson Loam: Front Cover Left and all other uncredited photos.
Commercial establishments contributing photos:
Beverly Hot Springs, Box Canyon Lodge, California Hot Springs, Desert Reef Beach Club, Elysium Institute, Esalen Institute, Family Hot Tubs, Faywood Hot Springs, Gila Hot Springs, Jemez Springs Bath House, Le Petit Chateau, Mono Hot Springs, Morningside Inn, Mountain Spaa Resort, Orvis Hot Springs, Puddingstone Hot Tubs, Sandpipers Holiday Park, Splash, Steamboat Springs, Strawberry Park Hot Springs, Sycamore Hot Springs, Ten Thousand Waves, Trimble Hot Springs, Vichy Hot Springs, Wheeler Hot Springs, White Sulphur Springs.

Hot Springs and Hot Pools of the Southwest

Copyright 1994 by Marjorie Gersh-Young

Revised edition 1994

Cartography, design, layout and production by Jayson Loam and Marjorie Gersh-Young

ISBN 0-9624830-6-0

Manufactured in the United States

Published by: AQUA THERMAL ACCESS
55 Azalea Lane
Santa Cruz, CA 95060

REGIONAL CONTRIBUTORS

DAVID BYBEE is the official keeper of the Orange County Sierra Club Singles Section "Hot Springs List", which is a decadent spoof of the highly competitive peak climbing lists, complete with is own point system, T-shirt, jacket patch and gold pin award. For information about the list send a $3.00 environmental conservation donation (to the Sierra Club) and a stamped SASE legal size envelope to *Keeper of the Hot Springs List,* 5322 Centinela Ave. Los Angeles, CA 90066-6908.

After many years of leading hot spring trips for Sierra Club members just for fun, Dave has now become a professional leader of group trips to geothermal soaking opportunities, and other phenomena, worldwide. For information about available trips, send a SASE to Hot Spring Odysseys at the address given above.

JUSTINE HILL is a travel writer/photographer/visual anthropologist who has traveled extensively and has written about and photographed other cultures, travel locations, sacred sites and the great outdoors. Committed to experiencing as much of life as possible, the first time she put on a backpack she climbed to the top of Mt. Whitney; on a challenge rode her three-speed bicycle from Santa Monica to San Diego; moved to Santa Fe, New Mexico for a year to experience the splendor of the Southwestern desert and its culture.

Justine has had an A-Z career. Although her BA from Barnard College/Columbia University is in English literature, the highlight of her college years was studying anthropology with Margaret Mead, who has been one of the most important teachers in her life.

She currently lives surrounded by nature in Topanga, California, where she has a stock of over 50,000 photos from across the country and around the world, which appear frequently in calendars, posters, magazines, postcards, travel literature and coffee-table books. For information about her photo collection and related services, contact Justine Hill at P.O. Box 608, Topanga, CA 90290. Phone: (310) 455-3409.

PHIL WILCOX, also known as "The Solar Man", is semi-retired and lives on a remote piece of land in Northern California. He loves to travel and has recently been seen in Alaska, Canada, Baja, Colorado, New Mexico and points west. When not traveling (often in search of hot springs) he designs, sells and installs remote home solar power systems. Send $3.00 for a complete solar catalog, or a SASE for basic information, to THE SOLAR MAN, 20560 Morgan Valley Rd., Lower Lake, CA 95457.

ROB WILLIAMS, age 41, has devoted his life to locating and soaking in the natural hot springs of Baja California. The discovery of natural hot springs has been his favorite pastime. Soaking in these wilderness spas offers great rewards. Rob likes to build hot tubs in remote areas. He has now developed a hot spring campground in Guadalupe Canyon.

Wherever Rob can find a dirt road or an old Indian trail he explores it. Northern Baja is his specialty. Four-wheel drive Jeeps are used to reach hidden, remote and wild canyons filled with palm forests and natural hot springs. Long hikes are rewarded with rejuvenating soaks in natural mineral water.

The best time of the year is winter and spring for driving and hiking to remote wilderness hot springs. The cooler temperatures make traveling Baja's dry land more pleasant.

For more information and reservations contact Rob's Baja Tours, P.O. Box 4003, Balboa, CA 92661. (714) 673-2670.

Hot Springs and Pools of the Southwest

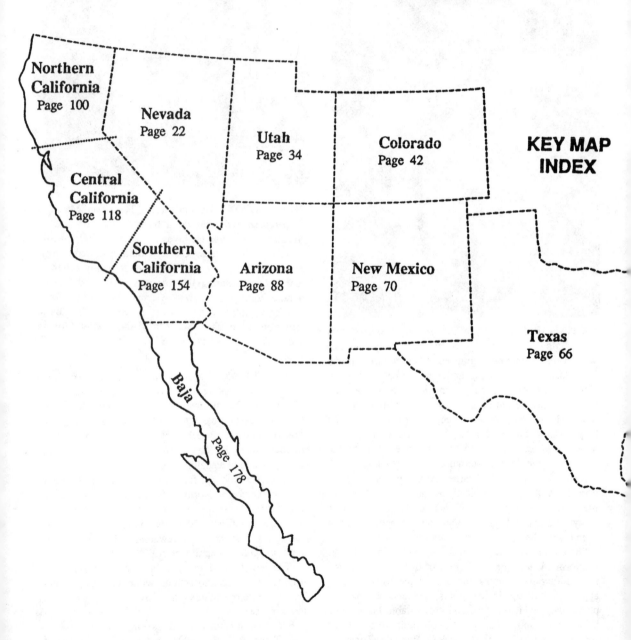

Northern California
Page 100

Nevada
Page 22

Central California
Page 118

Utah
Page 34

Colorado
Page 42

KEY MAP INDEX

Southern California
Page 154

Arizona
Page 88

New Mexico
Page 70

Texas
Page 66

Baja
Page 178

Table of Contents

This is a book for people to use, not an academic discussion of geothermal phenomena. For me there is a special joy and contentment which comes from soaking in a sandy-bottom pool of flowing natural mineral water, accompanied by good friends and surrounded by the peaceful quiet of a remote, primitive setting. At such an idyllic moment it is hard to get overly concerned about geology, chemistry or history. In this book it is my intent to be of service to others who also like to soak in peace and who could use some help finding just the right place.

The cataclysmic folding and faulting of the earth's crust over millions of years is a fascinating subject, especially where geologic sources have combined just the right amount of underground water with just the right amount of earth core magma to produce a hot surface flow that goes on for centuries. It would probably be fun to research and write about all that, including new data on geothermal power installations, but that is not what this book is about.

Many hot springs have long histories of special status with Indian tribes which revered the healing and peace-making powers of the magic waters. Those histories often include bloody battles with "white men" over hot spring ownership, and there are colorful legends about Indian curses that had dire effects for decades on a whole series of ill-fated owners who tried to deny Indians their traditional access to a sacred tribal spring. That, too, would be an interesting theme for a book someday, but not this book.

In the 19th century it was legal, and often quite profitable, to claim that mineral water from a famous spa had the ability to cure an impressive list of ailments. Such advertising is no longer legal, and modern medicine does not include mineral water soaks, or drinks, in its list of approved treatments. Nevertheless, quite a few people still have an intuitive feeling that, somehow, spending time soaking in natural mineral water is beneficial. I agree with the conclusion that it is "good for you", but it would take an entire book to explore all of the anecdotal and scientific material which would be needed to explain why. Someone else will have to write that book.

This book simply accepts the fact that hot springs do exist, that they have a history, and that soaking the human body in geothermal water does indeed contribute to a feeling of well-being. That still leave several substantial practical questions. "Where can I go to legally put my body in hot water, how do I get there, and what will I find when I arrive?" The purpose of this book is to answer those questions.

When I began to design this book, I had to decide which geothermal springs would be left out because they are not "hot". Based on my own experience I picked 90 degrees as the cut-off point and ignored any hot springs or hot wells below that level, unless a commercial operator was using electricity, gas or steam to bump up the temperature of the mineral water.

The second decision I had to make was whether or not to include geothermal springs on property which was fenced and posted or otherwise not accessible to the public. There are a few hot spring enthusiasts who get an extra thrill out of penetrating such fences and soaking in "forbidden" mineral water. It was my conclusion that I would be doing my readers a major disservice if I guided them into a situation where they might get arrested or shot. Therefore, I do not provide a descriptive listing for such hot springs, but I do at least mention the names of several such well-known locations in the index, with the notation NUBP, which means "Not Usable By the Public."

And then there were several more pleasant decisions, such as whether or not to include hot wells. Technically, they are not natural hot springs, but real geothermal water does flow out of them, so, if a soaking pool is accessible to the public, I chose to include them.

Within the last 30 years the radical idea of communal soaking in a redwood or fiberglass hot tub filled with gas-heated tap water has grown into a multi-million-dollar business. Thousands of residential tubs are installed every year, all of the larger motels and hotels now have at least one, and there are now dozens of urban establishments which offer private-space hot tub rentals by the hour. I chose to include rent-a-tub locations, which is why the book title is Hot Springs **and** Hot Pools.

Early on I realized that there is no such thing as a "typical" hot spring and that there is no such thing as a "typical" hot spring enthusiast. Some readers will have a whole summer vacation to trek from one remote, primitive hot spring to another. Others will be trying to make the most of a two week vacation, a long weekend, a Saturday, or a few hours after a hard day's work. Some readers will have a self-contained RV, while others must depend on air travel and airport transportation connections. Some readers will want to find skinnydippers, while others will want to avoid them.

Whatever your schedule, transportation and modesty needs, this book is intended to help you make an informed choice and then get you to the locations you have chosen.

Introduction
by Marjorie Gersh-Young

When I first discovered hot springs, my old and new values were waging internal war. Therefore, I was fascinated by the Indian tradition of declaring a hot spring to be a neutral zone, devoted to peace and healing rather than to conflict, and decided to follow their lead. How wonderful it is to immerse my body in a hot spring, or even in an urban hot tub, and declare it to be my personal neutral zone.

Gathering factual information for a book about hot springs required two summers and over 15,000 miles of travel. In the process it became my personal challenge to also make a subjective evaluation of which ones "felt the best," and to observe my mental impressions of the different kinds of people who frequent the springs.

At first, I applauded almost any type of geothermal soaking pool as being a gem of natural magic. As I visited more and different springs I gradually acquired a strong preference for rustic hikes to primitive pools fed by flowing springs, and a strong prejudice against crowded commercial resorts and chlorinated pools. I noticed that some traditional resorts advertise the unique mineral analysis of their geothermal water, but I am more interested in the water being clean, comfortably warm and free from "rotten egg" odors. I especially enjoy those natural soaking pools located next to a creek where it is possible to adjust the water temperature by moving a few rocks.

During my travels I developed a theory about why natural non-commercial hot springs felt so much more relaxing than commercial resort pools. At the natural pools there is no need to "maintain an image," and almost no way to do it, especially in a group of skinnydippers. It always amazed me that sitting in the same pool might be a lawyer and his wife who had driven up from town in a Cadillac; a family touring in a motorhome; and a group traveling around the area on their motorcycles. Some of us were "barefoot all the way," others had on bathing suits. The diversity was complete. Yet, here in the warmth of the water we were all soaking together in peace. Everyone's harmonious presence complemented the quiet beauty of a remote natural hot-spring pool.

Although I live many miles from the nearest hot spring, I have the benefit of two local rent-a-tub facilities which offer outdoor communal tubs surrounded by trees, grass and flowers, and a similar diversity of people. Such an arrangement is indeed almost as good as the real thing. If you can't be at the pool you love, love the pool you're at.

Buckeye Hot Spring: A unique early morning stillness. Steam rising off the hot rocks backlit with the rising sun. Sounds of the creek flowing and the occasional rustle of brush and the trill of birds. An experience I wish for every one of you.

Jayson Loam's life was a celebration of the things he loved to do based on what he called "having paid his dues." This meant that he had put in the time, often doing things he was not all that fond of, to gain both the knowledge and the funding to not commit the only sin in the world that he recognized-doing anything other than what you love to do. Researching hot springs and sharing his knowledge is what he loved to do best. And, he taught me to love it too. I have joyfully decided that the best way I can honor his life is to continue writing and publishing the hot springs books in the tradition he established so that all of you can continue to experience the best that was Jayson.

The above introduction was written for a previous edition. My original intent was to write a new one for this book, but as I sat down to do so and reread what I had written, I realized that my feelings had not changed, but indeed had been reinforced by all that I had seen and heard in the previous years. With all that is going on in the world it is still necessary to have places declared "neutral zones" where people from differing backgrounds and philosophies can come together.

May you soak in peace.
Marjorie

1. Hunting For Hot Water

Remington Hot Springs: This joyful soak on the banks of the Kern River depicts the wonderful feelings of soaking in natural mineral water out in nature where trees and birds add to the ambiance.

Long before the "white man" arrived to "discover" hot springs, the Indians believed that the Great Spirit resided in the center of the earth and that "Big Medicine" fountains were a special gift from The Creator. Even during tribal battles over camping area or stolen horses, it was customary for the sacred "smoking waters" to be a neutral zone where all could freely be healed of their wounds. Way back then, hot springs did indeed belong to everyone, and understandably, we would like to believe that nothing has changed.

Most of us also have a mental picture of an ideal hot spring. It will have crystal clear water, of course, with the most beneficial combination of minerals but with no slimy algae or rotten egg smells. Water temperature will be "just right" when you first step in, as well as after you have soaked for a while. It will occupy a picturesque rock-rimmed pool with a soft sandy bottom, divided into a shallow section for lie-down soaks and a deeper section for sit-up-and-talk soaks. Naturally, it will have gorgeous natural surroundings with grass, flowers and trees, plus an inspiring view of snow-capped mountains. The location will be so remote that you have the place to yourself, and can skinnydip if you choose, but not so remote that you might get tired from a long hike. Finally, if you like to camp out, there will be a lovely campground with rest rooms conveniently nearby or, if you prefer more service, a superior motel/restaurant just a short drive down the road.

Oh yes, this ideal spring will also be located on public land and therefore belong to everyone, just like all other hot springs. That leaves only the problem of finding that ideal spring, or, better yet, lots of them.

The "good book" for hot spring seekers is the *Thermal Springs List of the United States,* published by the National Oceanic and Atmospheric Administration and available through the NOAA Environmental and Data Service office in Boulder, Colorado. This publication contains nearly 1,600 entries, with nearly all of them in the eleven western states. For each hot spring entry, latitude, longitude, water temperature and the name of the applicable USGS quadrangle map are specified. The list is accompanied by a nice big map, sprinkled with colorful location dots.

This impressive package of official information has prompted more than one desk-bound writer to recommend and/or photocopy this list, implying that there is a publicly-owned, freely-available, idyllic, primitive hot spring under every dot; just buy your USGS map and go for it. Unfortunately, the real world of geothermal water is not quite that magical. We found that only seven percent of the listed springs are on public land, accessible without charge.

Our hot springs research program did start with an analysis of the NOAA springs list. We noticed that nearly one-third of the locations had temperatures below 90º, so we eliminated them as simply not being hot enough. The other two-thirds required individual investigation, usually involving personal inspection. In addition to the above-mentioned seven percent, we found that fifteen percent were private commercial enterprises, open to the public. All the rest were on posted private property, or otherwise not usable by the public.

Space does not permit reporting all of the reasons why various springs on the NOAA list are NUBP (not usable by the public). In some cases the NOAA data is 50 or 100 years old, and the spring has simply ceased to flow due to earthquake or heavy irrigation-well pumping. Some springs have been capped and fed into municipal water systems or drowned by the construction of a water reservoir. The largest single group of NUBP springs are those on non-commercial private property. Under our public liability laws, a hot spring's owner is practically forced to either operate a commercial establishment or post the property with NO TRESPASSING signs. An owner who had graciously permitted free public use of a hot spring for years had a user hurt himself on the property, file suit against the owner and collect damages. An owner's only defense against such suits is to fence and post the property, then show that the injured person was trespassing and therefore not legally entitled to blame the owner for anything.

Among the commercial hot spring establishments there is a very wide variety of facilities and services. Each business has developed over time as a unique combination of compromises between sometimes-conflicting influences, focused around what was once a primitive hot spring. The temperature and mineral content of the geothermal water flow, and the surroundings, determined the location and original character of the business, but European traditions, Victorian prudery, medical science advances, state health department pool regulations and changing recreation patterns have affected the merchandising of that mineral water.

The Indian tradition of free access to hot springs was initially imitated by pioneering palefaces. However, as soon as mineral water was perceived to have some commercial value, the new settler's private property laws were invoked at most of the hot spring locations, and the Indians were herded off to reservations. After many fierce legal battles, and a few gun battles, some ambitious settlers were able to establish clear legal titles to the properties. Then it was up to the new owners to figure out how to turn their geothermal flow into cash flow.

Pioneering settlers dismissed as superstition the Indian's spiritual explanation of the healing power of a

Although crowded in summer, skiing into *Grover Hot Springs* in the winter almost assures you of a private soak such as this young man is taking at *Ten Thousand Waves.*

hot spring. However, those settlers did know from experience that it was beneficial to soak their bodies in mineral water, even if they didn't know why or how it worked. Commercial exploitation began when the owner of a private hot spring first started charging admission, ending centuries of free access. Today, extracting a fee from the customer for the privilege of bathing in hot mineral water is still the fundamental transaction in the business. However, the fee you pay will seldom buy you an Indian-style soak, in a natural, free-flowing, sand-bottom hot spring in the wide open spaces. You are more likely to be offered a Victorian-style soak, in a one-person cast-iron tub in a small room in a men's or women's bathhouse, using mineral water piped in from a capped spring.

The shift from outdoor soaks to indoor soaks began when proper Victorian customers demanded privacy, which required the erection of canvas enclosures around the bathers in the outdoor springs. Then affluent city dwellers, as they became accustomed to indoor plumbing and modern sanitation, were no longer willing to risk immersion in a muddy-edged, squishy-bottom mineral spring, even if they believed that such bathing would be good for their health. Furthermore, they learned to like their urban comforts too much to trek to an outdoor spring in all kinds of weather. Instead, they wanted a civilized method of "taking the waters", and the great spas of Europe provided just the right model for American railroad tycoons and land barons to follow, and to surpass.

Around the turn of the century, American hot spring resorts fully satisfied the combined demands of Victorian prudery, modern sanitation and indoor comfort by offering separate men's and women's bathhouses, with private individual porcelain tubs, marble shower rooms and central heating. A scientific mineral analysis of the geothermal water was part of every resort merchandising program, which included flamboyant claims of miraculous cures and glowing testimonials from medical doctors. Their promotion material also featured additional social amenities, such as luxurious suites, sumptuous restaurants and grand ballrooms.

In recent decades, patronage of these resorts has declined and many have closed down because the traditional medical claims were outlawed and modern medical plans refuse to reimburse anyone for a mineral water "treatment". A few of the larger resorts have managed to survive by adding new facilities such as golf courses, conference and exhibition spaces, fitness centers and beauty salons. The smaller hot spring establishments have responded to modern demand by installing larger (six persons or more) communal soaking tubs and family-size soaking pools in private spaces for rent by the hour. Most locations continue to offer men's and women's bathhouse facilities in addition to the new communal pools, but most have discontinued the use of cast iron one-person bath tubs.

In addition to the privately-owned hot spring facilities,

Calistoga Spa, one of the many spas and resorts in this town of hot water, has something for everyone, from the very youngest to seniors who enjoy getting out of the direct sun to soak.

there are several dozen locations which are owned by federal, state, county or city agencies. States, counties and cities usually staff and operate their own geothermal installations. However, locations in the U.S. National Forests and National Parks are usually operated under contract by privately-owned companies. The nature and quality of the mineral water facilities offered at these publicly-owned, but privately-operated, hot spring locations varies widely.

Our hunt for hot water did not stop with the NOAA hot spring list. We tracked down dozens of unintentional hot wells, resulting from oil exploration drilling, or drilling for agricultural irrigation water. Some of those hot wells have turned into "hot spring resorts", even though there never was a natural mineral hot spring at the location. There are also dozens of intentional hot wells, such as the private wells which serve motels and mobilehome parks in the Desert Hot Springs area.

Although natural mineral water (from a spring or well) is required for a truly authentic traditional "therapeutic soak", there is a new generation of dedicated soakers who will not patronize a motel unless it has a hot pool. They know full well that the pool is filled with gas-heated tap water, containing no minerals, and treated with chlorine, but it almost as good as the real thing, and a lot more convenient. Space does not permit a listing of all such motels, or hotels, or health clubs. However, we chose to include in our hunt for hot water those locations which offer private space hot tubs for rent by the hour

According to California legend, the historic redwood tub was invented by a Santa Barbara group which often visited Big Caliente Hot Springs, in the nearby mountains at the end of a Forest Service gravel road. One evening a member of the group wished out loud that they could have their delicious outdoor communal soaks without having to endure the long dusty trips to and from the springs. Another member of the group suggested that a large redwood wine cask might be used as an alternate soaking pool in the city. It would not be the real thing, but it was worth a try, and it was a success. Over time, the pioneering group discovered that their backyard redwood pool needed more than just a gas-fired water heater. It also needs a circulation pump and a filter and chlorine treatments and seats for the people. Before long, other refugees from the long Big Caliente drive began to build their own group soaking pools from wine casks, and the communal hot tub era was born.

For many years, the very idea of men and women gathering together in the same tub, especially if they didn't wear proper suits, was perceived as California-style major moral decadence and was denounced accordingly. However, as the installation of residential hot tubs gradually became a major industry nationwide, public disdain turned into public acceptance and then into public demand. Designs for many new motels now include some deluxe suites, each containing its own private hot tub, complete with tile, skimmer, hydrojets, and temperature controls.

 The traditional rustic California redwood tub is still being used at *Shibui Gardens,* while this new edgeless swimming pool is definitely state-of-the-art at *Las Rosas Hotel* in Baja.

2. Using This Guide

▲ The variety of soaking experiences at *Sierra Hot Springs* includes this metal stock-watering tank which is just the right size for this party of four.

The primary tool in this guide is the KEY MAP, which is provided for each state or geographical subdivision. The KEY MAP INDEX, on the outside back cover, tells the page number where each of the KEY MAPS can be found. Each KEY MAP includes all significant cities and highways, but please note that it is designed to be used with a standard highway map.

Within every KEY MAP, each location has been assigned a number, which is imprinted next to the identifying circle or square. On the pages following the KEY MAP will be found the descriptions of each location, listed in numerical order.

The Master Alphabetical Index of Mineral Water Locations is printed at the end of the book, and gives the page number on which each location description will be found. If you know the specific hot spring name, this Alphabetical Index is the place to start.

If you are traveling in a geographical area and would like to know what hot spring or hot pool opportunities are available in that area, look at the KEY MAP for that area, note the likely location numbers and find the descriptions for those locations, by number, on the pages following the KEY MAP.

The following sections describe the quick-read symbols and codes which are used on the KEY MAPS and in the location descriptions.

Non-Commercial Mineral Water Locations

On the key maps in this book and in each hot spring listing, a solid round dot ● is used to indicate a non-commercial hot spring, or hot well, where no fee is required. At a few remote locations, you may be asked for a donation to help the work of a non-profit organization which has a contract with the Forest Service to protect and maintain the spring.

The first paragraph of each listing is intended to convey the general appearance, atmosphere and surroundings of the location, including the altitude, which can greatly affect the weather conditions. The phrase "open all year" does not mean that all roads and trails are kept open regardless of snowfalls or fire seasons. Rather, it means that there are no seasonally closed gates or doors, as at some commercial resorts.

The second paragraph describes the source and temperature of the mineral water and then conveys the manner in which that water is transported or guided to a usable soaking pool. "Volunteer-built pool" usually implies some crude combination of at-hand material such as logs, rocks and sand. If the situation requires that the pool water temperature be controlled, the method for such control is described. River-edge and creek-edge pools are vulnerable to complete washouts during high runoff months, so some volunteers have to start over from scratch every year.

The third paragraph identifies the facilities and services available on the premises, or nearby, and states the approximate distance to other facilities and services.

If needed, there is a final paragraph of directions, which should be used in connection with a standard highway map, a National Forest map if applicable, and any local area map which may be provided on the page near the listing.

With regard to skinnydipping, you had best start with the hard fact that any private property owner, county administration, park superintendent, or forest supervisor has the authority to prohibit "public nudity" in a specific area, or in a whole park or forest. Whenever a ranger has to deal with repeated complaints about nude bathers at a specific hot spring, it is likely that the area will be posted with NO NUDITY ALLOWED signs, and you could get a citation without warning by ignoring them. In a few places the National Forest rangers may be tolerant of clothing-optional preferences at non-posted hot springs, but the local county sheriff may arbitrarily decide to enforce a county ban on public nudity. Such county laws apply even within a National Forest.

The absence of NO NUDE BATHING signs does not necessarily establish the existence of a clothing-optional policy. Posted signs may have been torn down, or a forest-wide ban on public nudity may have been adopted but never posted. In any case the absence of a sign will at least give you the opportunity to explain to an officer that you had no desire to offend and that you are quite willing to comply with the rule, now that you know it exists.

At any unposted hot spring it is unlikely that you will be hassled for skinnydipping unless the officer is responding to a complaint. Therefore, you most important goal should be to make sure that there is no complaint. You may be pleasantly surprised at the number of people who are willing to agree to a policy of clothing-optional if, in a friendly manner, you offer them an opportunity to say yes.

Commercial Mineral Water Locations

On the key maps in this book and in the hot springs listings, a solid square ■ is used to indicate a natural mineral water commercial location. A phone number and mailing address are provided for the purpose of obtaining current rates, additional information and reservations.

The first paragraph of each listing is intended to convey the size, general appearance, atmosphere, and surroundings of the location, including the altitude. "Open all year" does not imply that the facility is open 24 hours of every day, only that it does not have a "closed" season.

A natural hot water shower feels good whether sitting under the ledges and caves at *Pah Tempe* or paddling down the East Carson river to get to *Riverside Hot Springs*, one of the two hot shower baths on or near the river.

Mud really seems to be the attraction both at *Glen Ivy* where, after you smear yourself thoroughly, you lay out on lounges and let the mud dry and crackle on your skin, and in the San Juan River, just below *Pagosa Springs*, where a dip in the river helps to remove all of the mud.

This book is about hot springs and hot pools where you can legally put your body in hot water. Therefore, the second paragraph of each listing focuses on the water and the pools available at the location. It describes the origin and temperature of the mineral water, the means of transporting that water, the quantity, type and location of tubs and pools, the control of soaking water temperatures, and the chemical treatment used, if any.

There actually are a few commercial locations where rare geothermal conditions (and health department rules) make it possible for a customer, or several, to soak in a natural sand-bottom hot spring open to the sky. On the other hand, there are several commercial locations which still operate separate men's and women's bathhouses fitted with traditional one-person cast-iron bathtubs. Most commercial locations fall in between these two extremes and offer a wide range of soaking opportunities.

Source hot springs are usually covered and the mineral water carried away in pipes, so customers seldom get to see a real spring, much less soak in one. Instead, the water is piped to the bathhouses for indoor use and also to swimming pools, soaking pools and hydrojet pools, usually outdoors and available for communal coed use. At a few large resorts the swimming and soaking pools may be located indoors, and some locations offer hydropools in private spaces for rent by the hour. In the last decade several resorts have also constructed special motel suites, each containing its own hydrojet pool.

In all states, health department standards require a minimum treatment of public pool water with chlorine, bromine or the equivalent. A few fortunate locations are able to meet these standards by operating their smaller mineral water pools on a continuous flow-through basis, thereby eliminating the need for chemical treatment. Many other locations meet these standards by draining and refilling tubs and pools after each use or after the end of each business day.

At those hot springs resorts which are being run as a business, bathing suits are normally required in public spaces. There are a few locations, usually operated by small special-interest groups, which have a policy of clothing-optional in the pools and sometimes everywhere on the grounds. If you are in doubt about the implications of such a policy, use the telephone to get answers to all of your questions.

The third paragraph of a commercial hot spring listing briefly mentions the principal facilities and services offered, plus approximate distances to other nearby services, and the names of credit cards accepted, if any. This information is intended to advise you if overnight accommodations, RV hookups, restaurants, health clubs, beauty salons, etc. are available on the premises, but it does not attempt to assign any form of quality rating to those amenities. There is no such thing as a typical hot spring resort and no such thing as typical accommodations at such a resort. Don't make assumptions; phone and ask questions.

For the quick-reference convenience of our readers, we

include some code letters in the headings of each listing:
PR = Tubs or pools for rent by hour, day or treatment.
MH = Rooms, cabins or dormitory spaces for rent by the day, week or month.
CRV = Camping or vehicle parking spaces, some with hookups, for rent by the day, week or month.

The PR code obviously applies to rent-a-tub establishments, and is also use for those hot springs resorts that admit the public to their pools on a day-rate basis.

The MH code covers every kind of overnight sleeping accommodation for rent, including tents and trailers as well as motel and hotel rooms, cabins and dormitories.

The CRV code is very general, indicating that there is dome kind of outdoor space in which some kind of overnight stay is possible. Some locations permit tents, most do not. Some have full hook-ups for RVs, most do not.

Tubs Using Gas-heated Tap Water or Well Water

In this book the listings of rent-a-tub locations begin with an overall impressions of the premises and the general locations, usually within a city area. This is followed by a description of their private spaces, tubs, and pools, water treatment methods, and water temperature policies. Generally, unless stated otherwise, clothing is optional in private spaces and required elsewhere. Facilities and services available on the premises are described, and credit cards accepted, if any , are listed. Nearly all locations require reservations, especially during the busy evening hours, and most employees are experienced at giving directions.

Nudist/naturist resorts which have hot pools are included as a special service to those who prefer to soak in the buff. It is true that most nudist/naturist resorts are not open to the public for drop-in visits but we wanted to give skinnydippers at least a few alternatives to all of the conventional motels/hotels/resorts which require bathing suits in all of their pools all of the time.. Most of the nudist/naturist resorts specifically prohibit bathing suits in their pools and have a policy of clothing-optional elsewhere on their grounds.

▲ *Murietta Hot Springs Resort*: This location is coded PR+MH, indicating day-use pool rental and motel or hotel rooms.

▲
▼ Whether it's a family picnic and swim at *Trimble Hot Springs* or privacy for two at *Sycamore Hot Springs*, hot mineral water adds to the pleasure of the day.

17

3. Caring For The Outdoors

Spence Hot Spring: This is how one wise
National Forest Supervisor resolved a
conflict over clothing between "naked
hippies" and "decent townfolk".

This is an enthusiastic testimonial and an invitation to join us in supporting the work of the U.S. Forest Service, the National Park Service, and the several State Park Services. At all of their offices and ranger stations we have always received prompt, courteous service, even when the staff was also busy handling many other daily tasks.

Nearly all usable primitive hot springs are in national forests, and many commercial hot spring resorts are surrounded by a national forest. Even if you will not be camping in one of their excellent campgrounds, we recommend that you obtain official Forest Service maps for all of the areas through which you will be traveling. Maps may be purchased from the Forest Service Regional Offices listed below. To order by mail, phone or write for an order form:

Rocky Mountain Region   (303) 236-9431
Wyoming, Colorado,
Nebraska, South Dakota
P.O. Box 25127   Denver, CO 80225

Intermountain Region   (801) 625-5354
Southern Idaho, Utah,
Nevada and Western Wyoming
324 25th St.   Ogden, UT 84401

Southwestern Region   (505) 842-3292
Arizona, New Mexico
517 Gold Ave. SW Albuquerque, NM 87102

Pacific Southwest Region.(415) 705-2874
California
630 Sansome St.   San Francisco, CA 94111

When you arrive at a national forest, head for the nearest ranger station and let them know what you would like to do in addition to putting your body in hot mineral water. If you plan to stay in a wilderness area overnight, request information about the procedure for obtaining wilderness permits and camping permits. Discuss your understanding of the dangers of water pollution, including giardia (back country dysentery) with the Forest Service staff. They are good friends as well as competent public servants.

The following material is adapted from a brochure issued by the Forest Service - Southwestern Region, Department of Agriculture.

DO NOT WASH IN STREAMS OR SPRINGS

Pour wash water on the ground away from streams and springs.

Wash yourself, your dishes and your clothes in a container, away from water sources.

Food scraps, tooth paste, even biodegradable soap will pollute streams and springs. Remember, it's your drinking water, too!

Try to pack out trash left by others. Your good example may catch on!

PACK IT IN — PACK IT OUT

Bring trash bags to carry out all trash that cannot be completely burned.

DON'T SHORT CUT TRAILS.

Trails are designed and maintained to prevent erosion.

Cutting across switchbacks and trampling meadows can create a confusing maze of unsightly trails.

Aluminum foil and aluminum lined packages won't burn up in your fire. Compact it and put it in your trash bag.

19

CAMPFIRES   Use gas stoves when possible to conserve dwindliing supplies of firewood.

Use only fallen timber for firewood. Even standing dead trees are part of the beauty of wilderness, and are important to wildlife.

If you need to build a fire, use an existing campfire site if available.

Clear a circle of all burnable materials.

Dig a shallow pit for the fire.

Keep the sod intact.

If you need to clear a new fire site, select a safe spot away from rock ledges that would be blackened by smoke; away from meadows where it would destroy grass and leave a scar; away from dense brush, trees and duff where it would be a fire hazard. Keep fires small.

Never leave a fire unattended.

Put your fire COLD OUT before leaving, by mixing the coals with dirt & water. Feel it with your hand. If it's cold out, cover the ashes in the pit with dirt, replace the sod, and naturalize the disturbed area. Rockfire rings, if needed or used, should be scattered before leaving.

DON'T BURY TRASH!

Animals dig it up.

BURY HUMAN WASTE

When nature calls, select a suitable spot at least 100 feet from open water, campsites and trails. Dig a hole 4 to 6 inches deep. Try to keep the sod intact.

Don't pick flowers, dig up plants or cut branches from live trees. Leave them for others to see and enjoy.

After use, fill in the hole completely burying waste and TP: then tramp in the sod.

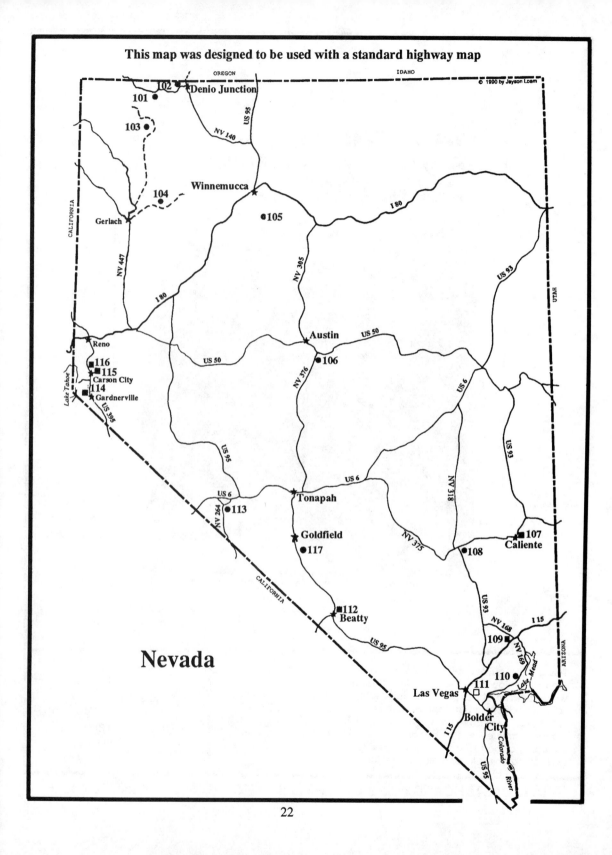

This map was designed to be used with a standard highway map

OREGON   IDAHO

© 1990 by Jayson Loam

102 Denio Junction

101

US 95

103

NV 140

104 Winnemucca

Gerlach   105

I 80

US 93

NV 305

NV 447

I 80

Austin   US 50

Reno

116   NV 376   106

115
Carson City

114
Gardnerville

US 395

US 50

US 6

US 95

US 93

US 6

NV 318

US 6

Tonapah

US 6

NV 264   113   Goldfield

117   NV 375   107
Caliente

108

Nevada

112
Beatty

US 93

NV 168   I 15

US 95   109   NV 169
ARIZONA

110

111
Las Vegas

Bolder
City

Colorado River

I 15

US 95

LAKE TAHOE

CALIFORNIA

CALIFORNIA

UTAH

Lake Mead

MAP AND DIRECTORY SYMBOLS

● Non-commercial mineral water pool

■ Commercial (fee) mineral water pool

☐ Gas-heated tap or well water pool

〜 Paved highway

− − − − Unpaved road

⋯⋯ Hiking route

PR = Tubs or pools for rent by hour, day or treatment

MH = Rooms, cabins or dormitory spaces for rent by day, week or month

CRV = Camping or vehicle parking spaces, some with hookups,
       for rent by day, week, month or year

---

101   VIRGIN VALLEY WARM SPRING

● **In the Sheldon Wildlife Refuge**

A charming, gravel-bottom warm pond, with an old adobe bathhouse in a small campground. Located in the high desert foothills near the Nevada-Oregon border. Elevation 5,100 ft. Open all year, subject to snow blockage on road.

Natural mineral water emerges up through the pond bottom (and is piped from other nearby springs) at 89º. The rate of flow maintains pond temperature at approximately 85º, depending on air temperature and wind speed. No chemical treatment is necessary. Bathing suits are required.

A continuous spring-fed shower at 88º is available in the adobe bathhouse and is a real treat for desert travelers. The campground is equipped with chemical toilets. Free camping is available. Services are available 27.5 miles away in Denio.

Directions: On NV 140, 27.5 miles west of Denio Junction and ten miles east of the Cedarville Road Junction, watch for a road sign *Virgin Valley, Royal Peacock Mine.* Go south on the gravel road 2.5 miles to campground.

Virgin Valley Warm Spring: After a long trek across the desert how wonderful to find a warm shower, a place to camp and soak at this oasis.

▲ *Bog Hot Springs*: The closer you walk to the head of this man-made channel the hotter the water. Wind also affects the water temperature.

▲ Close to a working ranch which offers bed and breakfast, this deep pond at *Soldier Meadow* presents a grand view of the open range.

102   BOG HOT SPRINGS

● **Near the town of Denio**

A large sand-bottom ditch carrying hot mineral water to an irrigation pond. Located on brush-covered flat land just below the Nevada-Oregon border. Elevation 4,300 ft. Open all year.

Natural mineral water flows out of several springs at 122º, is gathered into a single man-made channel, and gradually cools as it travels toward the reservoir. A dam with spillway pipe has been built at the point where the temperature is approximately 105º, depending on air temperature and wind speed. Around the dam, brush has been cleared away for easy access and nearby parking, but it is possible to soak in the ditch farther upstream if a warmer water temperature is desired. Clothing optional is probably the custom at this remote location.

There are no services available, but there is an abundance of level space on which overnight parking is not prohibited. It is 13.7 miles to a restaurant, store, service station, motel and RV hookups in Denio Junction.

Directions: From Denio Junction, go west on NV 140 for 9.2 miles, turn right and drive north for 4.3 miles on gravel road. Turn left and drive 100 yards to ditch and turn-around area.

103   SOLDIER MEADOW

● **North of the town of Gerlach**

Delightful deep pond located in the middle of a large meadow with a beautiful view of the surrounding desert and nearby Calico Mountains. Near High Rock Lake in the Black Rock Desert of northwest Nevada. Elevation 4,500 ft. Open all year.

Natural mineral water seeps up through the bottom of this natural sand and stone, five-and-a-half foot pond. The water temperature is approximately 102º. The apparent local custom is clothing optional.

There are no services available, but overnight parking is not prohibited. (Soldier Meadow Ranch near the spring is a private working ranch and bed and breakfast. Do not camp on their property.) It is 62 miles to a service station and mini-mart in Gerlach.

Directions: From Gerlach, take Hwy 34 north and east for 12.2 miles. Turn right on Soldier Meadow Road (mostly good gravel surface) for 50 miles. Bear left toward Summit Lake at first Soldier Meadow sign (Humboldt County Road #217). Turn left one mile at second Soldier Meadow sign. Proceed .2 mile to Spring.

Note: Upon leaving, there are numerous other hot springs on road to High Rock Lake, but a 4-wheel-drive vehicle is recommended and road is rough.

Trego Hot Ditch: The whistle from a passing train may be one of the only sounds you hear as you soak out in the middle of the desert.

104   TREGO HOT DITCH

● **South of the town of Gerlach**

A hot ditch next to Western Pacific railroad tracks. Located in the Black Rock Desert with a back drop of the Pahsupp Mountains. Elevation 4,000 ft. Open all year.

Natural mineral water flows out of the ground by the railroad tracks at 107º and cools gradually as it flows toward a small man-made dam. Wooden stairs lead down into the water where the temperature is 104º. Clothing is optional but pools can be seen from the tracks.

No services are available, but overnight parking is not prohibited. It is 20 miles to a service station and mini-mart in Gerlach.

Directions: From Gerlach, go 3 1/2 miles south on Route 447. Turn left on gravel county road #48 (no sign). Continue 17 miles and turn left toward railroad radio antenna. Continue 1 mile and turn right at the first fork, left at the second, and right at the third fork (antenna on left). Take the next left toward the railroad track (pool not visible).

●
Near the town of Winnemucca

The ultimate hard-luck hot spring trickling out of a barren mountainside. Elevation 4,500 ft. Open all year.

High-sulphur content mineral water flows out of the ground at 106º, and hot sulphur dioxide steam comes out of a nearby vent. At various times scrap lumber and other junk have been used by volunteers to enclose a soaking pit plus a "steam bath", and such structures have eventually been burned to the ground, adding another layer to the accumulated trash. Clothing optional is the apparent custom at this remote location.

There are no services available, but there is a limited amount of level space on which overnight parking is not prohibited. It is 18 miles to a store, restaurant and service station.

Directions: From Interstate 80, exit in Mill City onto NV 400 and go 16 miles south. Watch for *Kyle Hot Springs* sign, then go 11.2 miles east on a gravel road to the springs.

●
Near the town of Austin

A group of volunteer-built soaking pools on a knoll with a view of barren hills and snow-capped mountains. Elevation 5,700 ft. Open all year.

Natural mineral water flows out of several springs at 122º, then through a shallow channel down the slope of the knoll. Volunteers have dug a small soaking pool next to this channel and also installed a large metal stock tank for soaking. Water temperature is controlled by admitting only as much hot water as desired.

A second group of natural soaking pools is located several hundred yards further up the knoll. Natural mineral water with a faint sulphur smell bubbles up next to a metal casing in a shallow pool and flows through a volunteer-built rock channel into an adjoining 3-feet deep sand-bottom soaking pool. Water temperature can be controlled by adjusting the amount of hot water flow into the pool. A series of channels carries the water down the knoll into other pools. A wooden slat deck has been built near the largest soaking pool. Clothing optional is the apparent local custom at this remote location.

There are no services available but there is a limited amount of level space on which overnight parking is not prohibited. A steel fire pit has been built near the metal soaking tank, and there are several large bins for trash collection. Please do your part to keep this location clean.

Directions: From the intersection of US 50 and NV 376, go 100 yards south on NV 376, then go 5.5 miles southeast on a gravel road. Bear left on a dirt road which leads up the hot-spring knoll.

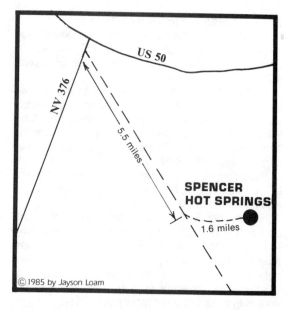

© 1985 by Jayson Loam

 This is largest of the man-made soaking pools dug along the channels which carry the hot mineral water from several source springs at *Spencer*.

Spencer Hot Springs: At this location thoughtful volunteers have provided picnic benches as well as several soaking pools.

107 CALIENTE HOT SPRINGS MOTEL
Box 216   (702) 726-3777
Caliente, NV 89008   PR+MH+RV

Primarily a motel, with some hot-water facilities. Located on the edge of Caliente in beautiful Rainbow Canyon, 150 miles north of Las Vegas. Elevation 4,400 ft. Open all year.

Natural mineral water flows from a spring at 115º and is piped to soaking pools. There are three indoor, family-size, newly retiled soaking pools in which hot mineral water and cold tap water may be mixed as desired by the customer. No chemical treatment is necessary because soaking pools are drained, cleaned and refilled after each use. Soaking pools may be rented by the public on an hourly basis; free to motel guests.

Six rooms with kitchenettes and a hydrojet tub using hot mineral water and cold tap water are available on the premises. Visa and MasterCard are accepted. A restaurant, store and service station are within a few blocks.

Directions: From the center of Caliente, go 1/2 mile north on US 93. Watch for signs and entrance road on east side of highway.

108   ASH SPRINGS

● **North of the town of Alamo.**

Tree-lined channels of warm geothermal water, surrounded by barren desert foothills. Elevation 4,000 ft. Open all year.

Hundreds of gallons per minute of natural mineral water flows out of several springs on Bureau of Land Management (BLM) property at 91° and gradually cools as it runs off though large sandy ditches. In the more secluded areas, clothing optional is the apparent local custom.

Within a few hundred yards, the BLM flow merges with the outflow of additional springs on adjoining private land (Ash Springs Resort), where it forms a large classic "Ye Olde Swimming Hole." Depending upon the current ownership and management of the resort, it might be open to the public, or might be available only to private club members, or closed. Do not enter the private land until you are sure you are not trespassing.

There are no facilities on the BLM land, but there is plenty of level area on which overnight parking is not prohibited. A service station, restaurant, store and campground are available in the commercial area across the highway.

Directions to BLM land pools: From Alamo on US 93, drive north four miles to Ash Springs Resort on the right side of the highway. Continue north beyond the end of the resort property fence and turn right on a narrow dirt road for 100 yards to an informal camping/campfire area and several adjoining soaking pools.

Ash Springs: Although "Ye Olde Swimming Hole" located on private property is often closed, other available soaking pools can be found on public BLM land

109　WARM SPRINGS RESORT

■　**Moapa, NV 89025**

(702) 865-27870

PR+CRV

A large RV oasis in the desert, with acres of grass and dozens of palm trees, blessed with a warm-water flow of 3,000,000 gallons per day. Located 50 miles north of Las Vegas. Elevation 1,800 ft. Open all year.

Natural mineral water flows out of several springs at 90º and runs through the grounds in a series of gravel-bottom pools and tree-lined channels. A large outdoor swimming pool uses mineral water on a flow-through basis, maintaining a temperature near 90º. The outdoor hydropool uses mineral water heated to approximately 101º and chlorine-treated. Bathing suits are required in both pools.

Facilities include a club house and men's and women's locker rooms. Pool use is available on a day-rate basis. RV hookups and camping spaces are available. Phone first for confirmed reservation. No credit cards are accepted.

There are no services available on the premises. It is nine miles to a store, restaurant, service station, etc.

Directions: From I-15, take NV 168 west for seven miles, then follow signs two miles west to resort.

▲　*Warm Springs Resort*: This always-warm swimming pool is too large to ever get crowded, even when the RV park is full.

▲　A combination massage and a soak can be had at one of the many waterfalls on the property at *Warm Springs Resort*.

Near the town of Overton

A refreshing warm pond and shady picnic oasis on the barren north shore of Lake Mead in the Lake Mead National Recreation Area. Elevation 1,600 ft. Open all year.

Natural mineral water at approximately 90º flows directly up through a gravel bottom into a 100-foot-diameter pool at a sufficient rate to maintain the entire three-foot-deep pool at approximately 80º. Hundreds of gallons per minute flow over a cement and rock spillway in a series of small waterfalls. Bathing suits would be advisable at this location in the daytime.

There are no services available, and overnight parking (after 10 P.M.) is prohibited. It is 8.5 miles to a store, restaurant and service station in Overton, and five miles to a campground.

Directions: From the intersection of US 93 and NV 147 in the city of Henderson, go northeast on Lake Mead Drive. At the intersection with Northshore Road (NV 169), follow Northshore Road northeast toward Overton. Rogers Warm Spring is four miles beyond the Echo Bay Marina turnoff.

Alternate Directions: When approaching from the north, take I-15 exit Logandale/Overton. Turn east on NV 169 to "Lake Mead National Recreation Area" and continue south for 27 miles to the ROGERS SPRING sign.

Rogers Warm Spring: Warm water flows up through the bottom and over this spillway into this huge pond at a true desert oasis

Rogers Warm Spring: Shaded picnic tables, rocks to climb, and a shallow warm pool make this a welcome break for families.

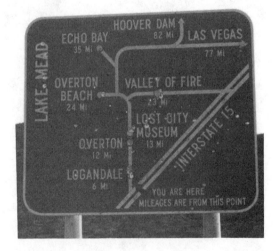

111 SPRING FEVER

3434 Boulder Hwy.   (702) 457-8000
☐ Las Vegas, NV 89005   PR

Modern rent-a-tub establishment located near downtown Las Vegas. Elevation 2,500 ft. Open all year, 24 hours.

Eighteen pools in private rooms are for rent to the public. Gas-heated tap water treated with chlorine is maintained at temperatures of 94-98º in the summer and 100-102º in the winter. Sauna and toilets are included in each room. Pools are rented on a first-come, first-served basis--no reservations.

A juice bar is on the premises. No credit cards are accepted. Phone for rates and directions.

112 BAILEY'S HOT SPRINGS

Box 387   (702) 553-2395
■ Beatty, NV 89003   PR+CRV

Primarily an RV park with three large, indoor hot mineral water soaking pools. Located in the high desert country just east of Death Valley National Monument. Elevation 2,900 ft. Open all year.

Natural mineral water emerges from an artesian well at 110º, and bubbles up through the gravel-bottoms of three indoor soaking pools which used to be railroad water reservoirs. Flow rates are controlled to maintain different temperatures in the three pools, approximately 101º, 105º and 108º. The rate of flow-through is sufficient to eliminate the need for chemical treatment of the water. Bathing suits are optional in private-space pools.

Overnight camping and RV hookups are available on the premises. No credit cards are accepted. It is six miles to a store and service station.

Directions: From the only traffic signal in Beatty, go 5 1/2 miles north on US 95. Watch for large sign on east side of road.

Fish Lake Hot Well: Volunteers have added this concrete soaking pool to the original small wood-lined soaking pit at the well.

113 FISH LAKE HOT WELL

● **Near the town of Dyer**

An inviting, cement-lined soaking pool on the edge of a truly remote barren desert wash in Fish Lake Valley, approximately half-way between Reno and Las Vegas. Winter is most beautiful, with snow-capped peaks encircling the valley. Elevation 4,800 ft. Open all year.

Natural mineral water emerges from a well casing at 105º and at a rate of more than 50 gallons per minute. The casing is surrounded by a six-foot by six-foot cement sump which maintains a water depth of four feet above a gravel bottom. From there it flows into a large cement soaking pool surrounded by a three-foot cement deck. The overflow goes to a nearby shallow pond used as a water supply for cattle. Clothing optional is the apparent custom at this remote location.

There are no services, and no shade trees, but there is an abundance of level space where overnight parking is not prohibited. Despite the fact that it is possible to drive within a few feet of the pool, it has been kept surprisingly clear of cans and broken glass. Please help keep it clean.

Directions: From the junction of NV 246 and NV 773, go 5.7 miles south on NV 264 to a gravel road on the east side of the highway. Follow this for seven miles to a fork, then bear left for 0.1 mile to springs. The gravel road is subject to flash-flood damage, so should not be attempted at night.

Source maps: USGS *Davis Mountain and Rhyolite Ridge* (well not shown on map).

31 NEVADA

114   WALLEY'S HOT SPRING RESORT
■ Box 26   (702) 782-8155
   Genoa, NV 89411   PR+MH

A self-styled "upscale destination resort" which attempts to present a nineteenth century resort image. Located 50 miles south of Reno at the foot of the Sierra. Elevation 4,700 ft. Open all year.

Natural mineral water flows from several wells at temperatures up to 160º and is then piped to the bathhouse and to six outdoor cement pools (two with jets) where the temperatures are maintained from 96-104º. The cement swimming pool uses bromine-treated creek water and averages 80º. Bathing suits are required in the outdoor pools.

The main building is a two-story health club with separate men's and women's sections each containing a sauna, steambath and weight training equipment. Massage is also available in each section. Facilities include rooms, dining-rooms and bars. Visa, MasterCard and American Express are accepted. It is seven miles to a store, service station and RV hookups.

Directions: From Minden on US 395, go 1/2 mile north to Muller Lane, turn west and go three miles to Foothill Rd., then 1/2 mile north to resort.

▼ In front of the restaurant building at *Walley's* are two of the soaking pools, all of which are have different temperatures.

▲ The indoor pools at *Carson Hot Springs* are roman-bath type soaking pits large enough to hold groups of six or more people.

115   CARSON HOT SPRINGS
■ 1500 Hot Springs Road   (702)882-9863
   Carson City, NV 89701   PR+RV

Older hot springs plunge with swimming pool and nine large private rooms, each containing a sunken tub large enough for eight persons. Located in the northeast outskirts of Carson City. Elevation 4,300 ft. Open all year.

Natural mineral water flows out of the ground at 126º. Air spray and evaporative cooling are used to lower this water temperature when pools are drained and refilled during each day. No chemical or city water is added. The outdoor swimming pool temperature is maintained at 98º in the summer and 102º in the winter. Individual room pool temperatures can be controlled as desired, from 95-110º. Bathing suits are required in the swimming pool, optional in the private rooms.

Massage, restaurant and no-hookup RV parking are available on the premises. Visa and MasterCard are accepted. It is one mile to a store and service station.

Directions: From US 395 at the north end of Carson City, go east on Hot Springs Road one mile to plunge.

Bowers Mansion: These well-maintained pools are part of a large recreation area built at a famous historical site.

Silver Peak Hot Spring: Makeshift soaking pools surrounded by debris are typical of abandoned old hot spring resort sites.

117   SILVER PEAK HOT SPRING

● **Near the town of Goldfield**

Two brick-lined soaking pools at the edge of a salt flat in the trashy remains of an abandoned turn-of-the century hot springs resort. Elevation 5,000 feet, Open all year.

Natural mineral water flows out of the ground through a flow pipe at 120º. On one edge of the source spring volunteers have used bricks to build two large (4-6 persons) soaking pools in which the temperature is controlled by diverting or admitting hot water as desired. Some people claim to enjoy the soak more when they close their eyes to block out the feeling of being in a city dump. The apparent local custom is clothing optional.

There are no services on the premises but there is plenty of level ground on which overnight parking is not prohibited. It is 11 miles to a store, service station, motel, etc.

Directions: From the town of Goldfield (27 miles south of Tonapah) drive north on US 95 for four miles and look for a sign to "Alkalai/Silver Peak" on the west side of the highway. Turn west and drive 6.8 miles on a rough paved road to a power sub-station. A large abandoned swimming pool is near the road, just past the power station. The soaking pools are up the hill beyond the station. This area can be very muddy after rain or snow.

116   BOWERS MANSION

4005 US 395 North   **(702)849-1825**
Carson City, NV 89704   **PR**

A Washoe County Park with extensive picnic, playground and parking facilities, in addition to a large modern swimming pool. Elevation 5,100 ft. Park open all year; pools open Memorial Day to Labor Day.

Natural mineral water pumped from wells at 116º is combined with cold well water as needed. The swimming pool and children's wading pool are maintained at 80º. Both pools are treated with bromine. Bathing suits are required. There is a charge for using the facilities.

There are no services available on the premises. Tours of the mansion are conducted from Mother's Day to the end of October. It is four miles to a restaurant, motel, service station and RV hookups.

Directions: Go ten miles north of Carson City on US 395. Watch for signs and turn west on side road 1 1/2 miles to location.

This map was designed to be used with a standard highway map

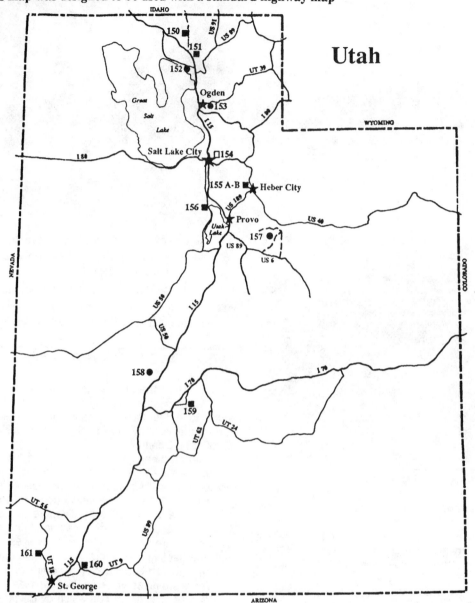

Utah

MAP AND DIRECTORY SYMBOLS

⬤ Non-commercial mineral water pool

◼ Commercial (fee) mineral water pool

☐ Gas-heated tap or well water pool

〜〜〜 Paved highway

– – – – Unpaved road

⋯⋯⋯ Hiking route

PR = Tubs or pools for rent by hour, day or treatment

MH = Rooms, cabins or dormitory spaces for rent by day, week or month

CRV = Camping or vehicle parking spaces, some with hookups,
for rent by day, week, month or year

▲ *Belmont Springs:* Much more than just a plunge, this location includes a golf course, an RV park and a recreation-oriented real estate development.

▲ *Crystal Hot Springs:* Tree-covered slopes, with shaded tenting areas, surround the giant waterslide, the large sunning lawns, and the user-friendly central pool area.

150   BELMONT SPRINGS
Box 36   **(801) 458-3200**
Fielding, UT 84311   **PR+CRV**

Modern, commercial plunge with RV park and golf course in a large northern Utah valley. Elevation 4,300 feet. Open April through October; scuba park open during winter.

Natural mineral water flows out of artesian wells at 125º and is piped to four outdoor pools, all of which are treated only minimally with chlorine at night, burning off by daytime. The large swimming pool is maintained at 93º, a hot-tub soaking pool at 106º, and two hot-tub hydrojet pools at approximately 106º. Bathing suits are required.

Locker rooms, two picnic areas, golf course, overnight parking and RV hookups, a scuba diving park and a tropical fish farm are available on the premises. A cafe, store, service station and motel are available within ten miles. Scuba instructors and classes are welcome. No credit cards are accepted.

Directions: From the town of Plymouth (exit 394) on I-15, go one mile south and watch for resort sign.

151   CRYSTAL HOT SPRINGS
8215 North Hwy 69   **(801) 279-8104**
Honeyville, UT 84314   **PR+CRV**

Superbly remodeled, historical resort featuring the world's largest side-by-side hot and cold springs. The property includes spacious, tree-shaded lawns for picnics and camping. Elevation 4,700 ft. Open all year.

Natural mineral water flows out of a spring at 135º and is piped to three outdoor hydrojet pools which are maintained at 102º, 104º and 106º on a flow-through basis requiring no chemical treatment. A large outdoor soaking pool of natural mineral water is maintained at 100º with a minimum of chlorine treatment. Another large soaking pool uses chlorine-treated spring water maintained at a temperature of 95º. Similar water is used in the catch-pool at the bottom of two large waterslides. There is also an Olympic-size swimming pool using cold spring water, which is drained and filled weekly and requires a minimum of chlorine treatment. Bathing suits are required.

Locker rooms, snack bar, overnight camping and RV hookups are available on the premises. It is four blocks to a store and service station and 15 miles to a motel. No credit cards are accepted.

Directions: From I-15, take Honeyville exit. Go one mile east on UT 240 to UT 69, then 2 1/2 miles north to resort on west side of highway.

 Stinky Springs: No one knows why this block house was built, or how it survives, but it continues to provide free soaks.

Ogden Hot Springs: This beautiful pool right on the river and not far from town seems to be a party place. Locals try to keep it clean.

152   STINKY SPRINGS

● **West of the town of Brigham City**

A small, partly vandalized cement-block bathhouse alongside a highway in the flat country north of the Great Salt Lake. Elevation 4,000 ft. Open all year.

Natural mineral water flows out of a spring at 118º, through a culvert under the highway, and into three cement soaking pits in the abandoned building. Temperature within each pool is controlled by diverting the hot-water flow as desired. In recent years volunteers have kept the surrounding party trash to a minimum, but the water does have a sulfur-dioxide smell. The apparent local custom is clothing optional within the building.

There are no services available on the premises.

Directions: From I-15, take the Golden Spike exit, then go nine miles west through Corinne on UT 83. The building is on the south side of the road shortly before you reach Little Mountain, a rocky hill on the north side of the road.

153   OGDEN HOT SPRINGS

East of the city of Ogden

Small, primitive hot spring at the river's edge located in a beautiful river gorge in Ogden Canyon. Elevation 4,800 ft. Open all year, subject to annual flooding.

Natural mineral water flows out of a spring at 130º and through a pipe and hoses to a volunteer-built, rock-and-mud pool at 107º. The water continues flowing into a rock-and-cement bottomed pool at 101º with the sides built up to prevent entrance of river water. The temperature is controlled by diverting the hoses when desired. The apparent local custom is clothing optional even though the highway is visible.

There are no services available on the premises.

Directions: Exit I-15 in Ogden at SR 39 (12th St.) and go east 4.9 miles to the mouth of Ogden Canyon. Park on either side of the road just after passing under suspended water pipe. Short trail downstream to spring starts at mile 9 green marker. (If pulling a trailer go one mile further upstream to a turn-around and come back to park.)

The Homestead: The proximity of Midway to several major ski slopes makes this indoor pool a popular wintertime attraction.

Mountain Spaa Resort: The indoor pool built in a large natural crater is now in the building beyond the swimming pool.

154 THE SPA CENTER (SOAK YOUR BODY)

3955 S. State St.   (801) 264-TUBS
☐ Salt Lake City, UT 84107   PR

Basic rent-a-tub establishment, plus spa sales and service, on a main street in southern Salt Lake City.

Private-space hot pools using bromine-treated tap water are for rent to the public by the hour. Six indoor, fiberglass hydrojet pools are maintained at temperatures ranging from 102-104º. Visa and MasterCard are accepted. Phone for rates, reservations and directions.

155A THE HOMESTEAD

700 N. Homestead Road (801) 654-1102
■ Midway, UT 84049   PR+MH+C

Remodeled, historic resort specializing in leisure vacations and group meetings, with extensive landscaping and a minimal use of natural mineral water. Elevation 5,600 ft. Open all year.

Natural mineral water flows from a tufa-cone spring at 92º where the water temperature is boosted and is piped to one small outdoor soaking pool which averages 100º and is not treated with chemicals. All other pools use chlorine-treated tap water. The large outdoor swimming pool is maintained at 85º, the indoor hydrojet pool at 98º, and the indoor lap pool at 90º. There is also a dry sauna available. Pool use is available to registered guests only. Bathing suits are required.

Locker rooms, dining rooms, and hotel rooms are available on the premises. It is two miles to a store, service station, RV hookups and a golf course. Visa, American Express and MasterCard are accepted.

Directions: From Heber City on US 189, go west on UT 113 to the town of Midway and follow signs to resort.

155B MOUNTAIN SPAA RESORT

800 North 200 East   (801) 654-0721
■ Midway, UT 84049   PR+MH+CRV

Historic resort, located in beautiful Heber Valley, one mile from Wasatch Mountain State Park. Elevation 5,700 ft. Open daily from Memorial Day to Labor Day, and during April, May, September and October, weather permitting..

Natural mineral water flows from cone-shaped tufa craters at 110º and is piped to two pools. The outdoor swimming pool, with kiddie slide and large deck area, is maintained at 90-95º. The indoor swimming pool is built inside a large crater, maintains a temperature of 95-100º. Both pools are drained twice weekly, disinfected and refilled.

Guest house, cabins, soda fountain, snack bar, game room, locker rooms, lawn and picnic area, overnight camping and RV hookups are available on the premises. Banquet room and pavillion facilities available for large groups. Visa and MasterCard are accepted.

Directions: From Heber City on US 189, go west on UT 113 to the town of Midway. Turn north on River Road, go .7 mile to 600 North in Midway and follow signs to resort.

▲ *Diamond Fork Hot Springs:* One of those idyllic spots in nature. You can even walk behind the waterfall.

157   DIAMOND FORK HOT SPRINGS
(also known as Fifth Water Canyon)

● **Spanish Fork, UT (South of Provo)**

Three volunteer-built rock pools in a beautiful canyon at the end of an easy hike, with its own flowing creek and large waterfall. Elevation 5,800 ft. Open all year subject to snow.

Natural mineral water flows out of the ground at 125º, and by moving rocks along the creek, combines with creek water to cool the higher pool to a comfortable temperature. The lower pool receives the overflow from the upper pool and is slightly cooler. The third pool is across the creek and is quite hot when the creek is low, but cools some when creek water is high and can flow over into pool. The apparent local custom is clothing optional.

There are no services available on the premises, but overnight camping is not prohibited at the trailhead and at the many pull-out spots along the creek. It is 15 minutes to a mini-mart in Spanish Fork.

Directions: From the junction of SR 89 and SR 6 (off I-15 south of Provo) proceed south on SR 6 for 6.2 miles. Turn left on paved road (Diamond Fork) and drive exactly 10 miles (passing many nice camping sites) to trailhead parking area. Cross bridge and start up trail. Stay straight and do not turn right over the second bridge. Cross the bridge over the creek. After 1 mile proceed another 1 1/2 miles slightly uphill on a well-maintained trail along Fifth Water Canyon to spring and waterfall.

▲ *Saratoga Resort:* This giant waterslide is the most popular of many attractions at this famous lakeside hot springs resort.

156   SARATOGA RESORT
Saratoga Rd. at Utah Lake

■ **Lehi, UT 84043**
(801) 768-8206
PR+CRV

Lakeside recreation resort with picnic grounds, rides and boat-launching facilities. Elevation 4,200 ft. Open May to September.

Natural mineral water is pumped out of a well at 120º and is piped to four outdoor pools, all of which are treated with chlorine. One large hydrojet pool is maintained at 100º. The swimming pool, diving pool and waterslide catch pool are maintained at 75-80º. Bathing suits are required.

Locker rooms, snack bar, overnight camping and RV hookups are available on the premises. There are also several amusement park rides. No credit cards are accepted.

Directions: From the town of Lehi on I-15, go west on UT 73 and follow signs to resort.

▲ *Meadow Hot Springs:* Holding on to the ropes, float out to the middle and look down through the clear water to the bottom.

▲ *Mystic Hot Springs:* Pick berries, soak in the healing water and view the natural warm water caves--just some of the activities available.

158   MEADOW HOT SPRINGS

● **South of Provo, near Meadow**

Delightful large rock pool with ample sitting room on underwater stone ledges. Located in the pasture lands of Utah with unobstructed views of the Pahvant Mountain Range. Elevation 4,800 ft. Open all year.

Natural mineral water flows up through the bottom of a beautifully clear, room-sized pool, at 100º. Several heavy ropes across the pool allow you to remain on the surface while viewing the clear, deep portions of the pool. The apparent local custom is clothing optional.

There are no facilities on the premises but overnight parking is not prohibited. It is six miles to a store in Meadow.

Directions: From I-15 (south of Provo) take exit #158 at Meadow. Turn east under freeway. Continue 1.6 miles. Turn right on gravel road. Continue west over freeway. Cross two cattle guards at 5 miles on gravel road. Turn left into parking area. Spring is about 200 yards south.

159   MYSTIC HOT SPRINGS OF MONROE

■ **575 East First North   (801) 527-4014**
Monroe, UT 84754   PR+CRV

RV park with restaurant, swimming pool, razzleberry campground and hillside soaking pool overlooking a green agricultural valley. Elevation 5,500 ft. Open all year.

Natural mineral water flows out of a spring at 168º, cooling as it flows across the mountains into a soaking pool where the temperature ranges from 100-105º. The water then flows on to the natural tropical fish ponds. Bathing suits are required.

Biking and hiking trails, store, picnic area, camping, full RV hookups, teepees and a sweat lodge are available on the premises. It is a short walk to the large and colorful Red Hill Spring, the natural warm water caves, and to the adjoining tropical fish pond. A service station is within four blocks. No credit cards are accepted.

Directions: From the town of Richfield on I-70, go six miles south on US 89, then three miles on UT 118 to the town of Monroe. Follow signs to resort.

Pah Tempe mineral water cascades into the shallow Virgin River, which becomes a giant run-and-splash family playground.

▲ ▼ *Pah Tempe Hot Springs:* Comfortable soaking pools have been constructed in the caves and on the ledges above the Virgin River.

160   PAH TEMPE HOT SPRINGS RESORT

825 North 800 East   (801) 635-2879
                                              635-2353

■   **Hurricane, UT 84737   PR+MH+CRV**

A secluded bed and breakfast health resort, featuring a spectacular flow of geothermal water out of the sides and bottom of the Virgin River canyon, 20 miles southwest of Zion National Park. Elevation 3,000 feet. Open all year; reservations required.

Natural mineral water flows out of rock grottos and up out of the riverbed at temperatures of 105-110º. There is one shaded, outdoor swimming pool which averages 98º. The four riverbank soaking pools range from 102-106º, and the two private indoor hydrojet pools average 105º. (Rebuilding of some of the river bank soaking pools is taking place following the 1992 earthquake.) The flow-through rate in all pools is sufficient to eliminate the need for chemical treatment of the water. Bathing suits are required; alcohol and smoking are prohibited.

Bed and breakfast accommodations, camping and full RV facilities, picnic tables, and vegetarian meals are available on the premises. Also available is the whirlpool center and Reiki massage therapy. It is one mile to a cafe, store and service station in the town of Hurricane. Visa and MasterCard are accepted.

Directions: From the town of Hurricane, go one mile north on UT 9 and follow signs to resort.

Note: Because of some significant man-caused damage to the aquifer we must limit the number of people per day. We are open by advanced pre-paid reservation only. Please call for update and reservations.

Veyo Resort: Nothing fancy - just a warm pool with dressing rooms, a snack bar, and shaded picnic tables next to a stream.

161   VEYO RESORT
750 East Veyo Resort Rd.(801) 574-2744
Veyo, UT 84782   PR

Older community plunge and picnic park with a small running stream. Elevation 4,600 ft. Open end of March to Labor Day.

Natural mineral water flows out of an artesian well at a temperature of 98º. There is one outdoor swimming pool which is chlorinated and maintains a temperature of 85º. Bathing suits are required.

Locker rooms, snack bar, volleyball court and picnic area are available on the premises. It is one mile to a store and service station, eight miles to overnight camping and RV hookups, and 12 miles to a motel. No credit cards are accepted.

Directions: From the city of St. George on I-15, go 19 miles north on UT 18 to the town of Veyo and follow signs to the resort.

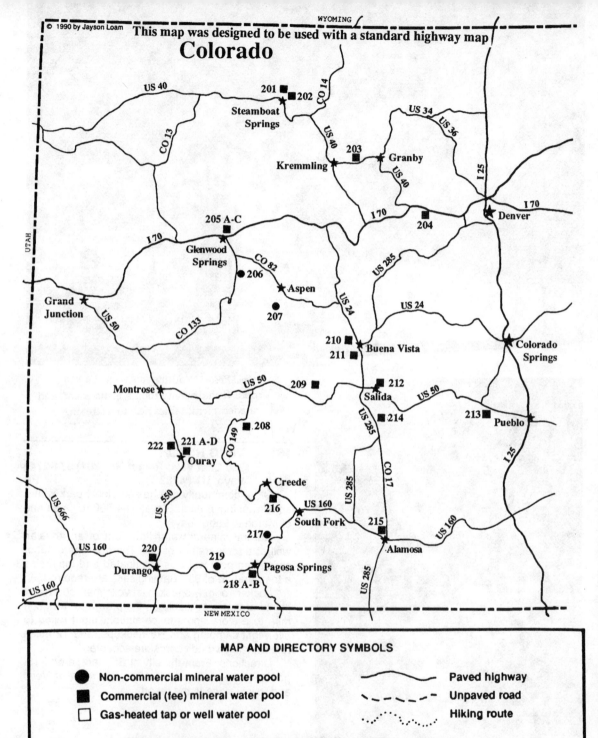

This map was designed to be used with a standard highway map
Colorado

WYOMING

UTAH

US 40

CO 13

201 202

Steamboat Springs

CO 14

US 40

US 34
US 36

203

Kremmling

Granby

I 25

205 A-C

I 70

Glenwood Springs

CO 82

206

Aspen

207

Grand Junction

US 50

CO 133

I 70

204

Denver

I 70

US 285

US 24

US 24

210
211

Buena Vista

Colorado Springs

Montrose

US 50

209

212

Salida

US 50

214

213

Pueblo

I 25

208

CO 149

222

221 A-D

Ouray

US 550

Creede

216

US 160

South Fork

US 285

CO 17

US 666

217

219

US 160

220

Durango

218 A-B

Pagosa Springs

215

Alamosa

US 160

US 285

NEW MEXICO

MAP AND DIRECTORY SYMBOLS

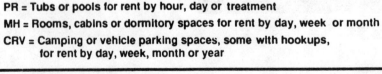

● Non-commercial mineral water pool   Paved highway

■ Commercial (fee) mineral water pool   Unpaved road

□ Gas-heated tap or well water pool   Hiking route

PR = Tubs or pools for rent by hour, day or treatment

MH = Rooms, cabins or dormitory spaces for rent by day, week or month

CRV = Camping or vehicle parking spaces, some with hookups, for rent by day, week, month or year

Strawberry Park Hot Springs: A masonry dam and an adjustable gate make it possible to mix geothermal and creek water as desired.

201 STRAWBERRY PARK HOT SPRINGS
P.O. Box 77332 (303) 879-0342
Steamboat Springs, CO 80477

PR+MH+CRV

A unique hot spring which manages to retain a maximum of primitive naturalness while improving the services for a variety of hot-spring enthusiasts. Elevation 7,500 ft. Open all year.

Natural mineral water flows out of many hillside fissures at 146º and cools successively as it is channeled into a series of creek-bank, rock-and-masonry pools where it is combined with creek water to provide a range of soaking temperatures (from 100-105º in the upper pool down to 85º in the lower pool). Continuous flow-through in all pools eliminates the need for chemical treatment. Bathing suits are required during the day (10 AM until dark); optional at night.

Cabins, overnight camping and catered private parties are available on the premises. Massage is also available. A bathhouse provides showers for overnight guests and cold drinks can be purchased.. It is seven miles to all other services. No credit cards are accepted.

Directions: From US 40 in the town of Steamboat Springs, go north on 7th St. and follow signs seven miles to location at the end of County Road #36. The steep grades are not recommended for trailers. Four wheel drive or tire chains are required on all vehicles during the winter season. Phone for hours, rates, reservations and transportation from Steamboat Springs.

One of the prettier places to soak at *Strawberry Park* is in this pool with views up and down the river.

43 COLORADO

202 STEAMBOAT SPRINGS
HEALTH AND RECREATION

P.O. Box 1211   (303) 879-1828
Steamboat Springs, CO 80477   PR

Large community plunge, hot pool, water slide and sauna near the city center. Elevation 6,700 ft. Open all year.

Natural mineral water flows out of a spring at 103º and is piped to five pools which are treated with chlorine. The soaking pool is maintained at a temperature of 101º, the water slide pick-up pool at 90º, and the large lap pool at 80º. Two large outdoor hydrojet pools are maintained at 102º. Bathing suits are required.

Facilities include locker rooms, saunas, snack bar, weight room, cardiovascular equipment and tennis courts. Exercise classes, massage, and child care are available on the premises. It is three blocks to a cafe, store, service station and motel, and two miles to overnight camping and RV hookups. Visa and MasterCard are accepted.

Location: On the north side of US 40, at the east edge of the city of Steamboat Springs.

Steamboat Springs is one of the few publicly-owned community geothermal plunges which has added a super slide.

There are many nippy mornings at *Steamboat Springs* when all of the pools are shrouded in a magical white cloud of steam.

203 HOT SULPHUR SPRINGS

P.O. Box 275   (303) 725-3306
Hot Sulphur Springs, CO 80451
PR+MH+CRV

Older resort located on US 40, which winds through the Rocky Mountains. Elevation 7,600 ft. Open in summer.

Natural mineral water flows out of a spring at 115º and is piped to a variety of pools. The outdoor swimming pool is treated with chlorine and maintained around 80º. Two outdoor soaking pools are maintained at 100-108º on a flow-through basis that eliminates the need for chemical treatment. There are two indoor pools in private spaces that rent by the hour, and there are two indoor pools in separate men's and women's bathhouses. Temperatures in these pools are 110º. Bathing suits are required except in indoor pools.

Dressing rooms, motel rooms, and picnic area are available on the premises. A free campground on the river is located adjacent to the property. It is three blocks to a cafe, store and service station, and 17 miles to RV hookups. No credit cards are accepted.

Directions: From US 40 in the town of Hot Sulphur Springs, follow signs north across the bridge to the resort.

▲ *Hot Sulphur Springs:* The variety of indoor and outdoor pools available attracts a wide range of mineral water customers.

Behind the main lodge at *Hot Sulphur Springs* is this pool with a cave, fed by water flowing over the bank through a pipe and preferred by many soakers who enjoy a natural feeling when they soak.

▼

Indian Springs Resort: A tropical garden has grown up under this famous translucent roof covering the large main pool.

204   INDIAN SPRINGS RESORT

P.O. Box 1300   (303) 623-2050
Idaho Springs, CO 80452   PR+MH+CRV

Popular historic resort just off I-70 in the Arapaho National Forest. Elevation 7,300 ft. Open all year.

Natural mineral water flows out of three underground springs at 124º. Within the men's cave are three walk-in soaking pools ranging in temperature from 104-112º. Within the women's cave are four similar pools. There are 11 private-space soaking pools outdoors, and four private-space tubs indoors large enough for couples or families, with temperatures of approximately 104°. All of the above pools operate on a flow-through basis so that a minimum of bromine is added. A minimum of bromine treatment is also used in the large, landscaped indoor pool, which is maintained at 96º in the winter and 90º in the summer. Bathing suits are required in the swimming pool and prohibited in the caves.

Mud baths, locker rooms, massage, dining room, hotel rooms, overnight camping and RV hookups are available on the premises. It is five blocks to a store and service station. Visa and MasterCard are accepted.

Directions: From I-70, take the Idaho Springs exit to the business district, then follow signs south on Soda Springs Road to resort.

205A   GLENWOOD HOT SPRINGS LODGE AND POOL

P.O. Box 308   (303) 945-6571
Glenwood Springs, CO 81601   PR+MH

A very large commercial resort near the center of town on the north bank of the Colorado River. Elevation 5,700 ft. Open all year.

Natural mineral water flows out of a spring at 130º and is mixed with cold spring water to supply four pools, all of which are treated with chlorine. The two-block-long swimming pool is maintained at a temperature of 90º, the outdoor soaking pool, with jet therapy chairs at 104º, the water slide catch-pool at 85º, and the indoor hydrojet pool (in the athletic club) at 104º. There is also a sauna and steambath in the athletic club. Bathing suits are required everywhere.

Locker rooms, cafe, hotel rooms and miniature golf course are available on the premises. It is one block to a store and service station and two miles to overnight camping and RV hookups. Visa, MasterCard, Diners Club, Discover and American Express are accepted.

▲ *South Canyon Springs* has had a rocky history of being open and closed. At this time all seems to be as peaceful as the scenery.

▲ *Glenwood Hot Springs Lodge and Pool*: This two-block-long pool complex can accommodate hundreds of day-use and lodge customers and still have room enough for a swim meet.

205B YAMPAH SPA
■ 709 E. 6th   (303) 945-0667
Glenwood Springs, CO 81601

Unique health center, one block from the large Hot Springs Lodge complex. Elevation 5,700. Open all year.

Natural mineral water creates vapor which emerges at 115º within three caves. All caves are coed and bathing suits are required. There are also two private-space hydrojet pools, filled with tap water, treated with chlorine, maintained at 104º.

Locker rooms, massage, facials, herbal wraps, rubs, body mud and reflexology are available on the premises. It is three blocks to a cafe, store, service station and motel, and five miles to overnight camping and RV hookups. Visa and MasterCard are accepted.

205C SOUTH CANYON SPRINGS
● **West of Glenwood Springs**

A primitive city-owned geothermal springs with a long history of controversy involving nudity and dynamiting of volunteer-built pools. Located in a narrow wooded canyon leading south off of the Colorado River. Elevation 5,200 ft. Open all year.

Natural mineral water flows out of the ground at 118° cooling as it flows to approximately 107° into four rock-and-sand pools, two on the creek and two up on the hillside across from the creek. The area is not currently fenced or posted and there is no recent pattern of harassment. The local custom is clothing optional.

There are no services on the premises but overnight parking is not prohibited.

Directions: From Glenwood Springs take I-70 to the South Canyon exit (#111), cross the Colorado River, cross the railroad tracks, and go up canyon .6 miles. Park along the west bank at pull out. Trail starts at north end of pull out and goes through woods for about 100 yards (take left fork at Y) to creek. First pool is directly across creek by small waterfall; larger and best pool up hill behind first pool.

206   PENNY HOT SPRINGS

● **North of the town of Redstone**

Primitive, riverbank hot spring seasonally flooded by high water. Elevation 8,000 ft. Open all year (subject to flooding).

Natural mineral water flows out of a spring at 133º and drops directly into the Crystal River. In between annual high-water washouts, volunteers build rock-and-sand pools in which hot mineral water and cold river water can be mixed to a comfortable soaking temperature. The location is close to the highway, so bathing suits are strongly recommended.

There are no services on the premises. All services are within three miles in the historic mining town of Redstone.

Directions: From Glenwood Springs heading toward Redstone, on the east side of CO 133, 0.8 miles south of mile marker 56, there is a small parking area on the east side of the highway next to the river. A short obvious trail goes down to the pools,   visible   from   the   embankment.

 Penny Hot Springs: Mom gets to relax and enjoy a soak in the warm water while the kids get to play on the rocks and in the river.

207   CONUNDRUM HOT SPRINGS

● **South of the town of Aspen**

Two primitive pools surrounded by spectacular Rocky Mountain scenery in a designated Wilderness Area of the White River National Forest. Elevation 11,200 ft. Open all year.

Natural mineral water flows out of a spring at 100º into two volunteer-built, rock-and-sand pools. The trail is so popular that the spring may be crowded. A long rugged climb will not necessarily give you quiet solitude. The local custom is clothing optional.

There are no services on the premises. It is eight miles of trail and five miles of rough road to a campsite. It is 20 miles to all other services.

This is a rewarding but hazardous location. Be sure to obtain directions, instructions and information about current trail conditions at a White River National Forest ranger station before attempting the trip.

Waunita Hot Springs Ranch: Thanks to an abundance of flow-through geotheremal water, this swimming pool requires a minimum of chlorine treatment.

208 YOUMANS STORE & CABINS (CEBOLLA HOT SPRINGS)
County Road 27   (303) 641-0952
Powderhorn, CO 81243   MH

Something special. An old-fashioned soak in a plank-lined spring covered by an authentic log cabin on a rugged mountain slope in central Colorado. Elevation 8,100 ft. Open May to October.

Natural mineral water flows out of two springs at 106° directly up through the bottom planks of two wood-lined pits which have been built within each spring. The odorless geothermal water flows through continuously, maintaining a pool temperature of 105° and eliminating the need for any chemical water treatment. There are no hydrojets, but you will feel an occasional gas bubble rising to the surface as you soak in natural silence. The soaking pools and cabin floor are kept very clean, and one of the cabins has a wood stove. Bathing suits are not required within the cabins. These hot springs are reserved primarily for the use of registered guests in the nearby rental cabins.

IMPORTANT NOTICE: At time of publication the previous owner had died and the property was up for sale so it is imperative that you phone ahead to determine the status of this location before attempting to drive to this remote location.

A store, service station, rental cabins and fishing are available on the premises. It is ten miles to a cafe and overnight camping and 20 miles to RV hookups. No credit cards are accepted.

Directions: From US 50 ten miles west of Gunnison, drive south on CO 149 approximately 15 miles and watch for Powderhorn turn off on left.

209 WAUNITA HOT SPRINGS RANCH
8007 County Road 887   (303) 641-1266
Gunnison, CO 81230   MH

American-plan guest ranch surrounded by Gunnison National Forest. Elevation 9,000 ft. Open all year.

Natural mineral water flows out of several springs at 175° and is piped to a swimming pool and to geothermal heating units in the buildings. The swimming pool is maintained at 95° and operates on a flow-through basis, so only a minimum of chlorine treatment is needed. Pool use is reserved for registered guests, with a minimum stay of six days by prior reservation only. Bathing suits are required.

Guest-ranch services, including rooms, meals, saddle horses and fishing, are available on the premises. It is 15 miles to a store, service station and overnight camping, and 28 miles to RV hookups. No credit cards are accepted.

Directions: From the town of Gunnison, go 19 miles east on US 50, then follow signs eight miles north to the ranch.

210　COTTONWOOD HOT SPRINGS INN

18999 Hwy 306　　　　**(719) 395-6434**
■ **Buena Vista, CO 81211**　　　　**PR+MH**

A small, rustic resort nestled in a high mountain valley, surrounded by the San Isabel National Forest. Elevation 8,500 ft. Open all year.

Odorless natural mineral water flows out of a well at 187º, cools to 120º in the 600-foot main conduit and is piped to three outdoor private-space hydrojet pools on a deck overlooking Cottonwood Creek. Individual pool temperatures range from 104-112º on a flow-through basis that requires no chemical treatment. Bathing suits are optional within the fenced private spaces. All pools are available to the public as well as to registered guests.

The mineral water is so pure that it is used as tap water throughout the resort. Facilities include spas and saunas, dressing rooms, three creekside cabins, 12 lodge rooms, camping teepees, Jump Steady Restaurant, meeting rooms and an exercise room. Massage is available by appointment. Visa and MasterCard are accepted. It is 5 1/2 miles to all other services.

The rustic setting and facilities are well-suited to small seminar groups, reunions, retreats, etc. Phone or write for rates and reservations.

Directions: From US 24 in Buena Vista, go west 5 1/2 miles on CO 306, the road to Cottonwood Pass. Watch for resort signs on the right side of the road.

Cottonwood Hot Springs Inn: Colorful urban-type fiberglass soaking tubs have been installed on rustic outdoor decks overlooking a mountain stream which runs all year.

▲
►
Mount Princeton Hot Springs: In addition to a regular swimming pool there is this shallower family play pool where adults can stand on the bottom when they choose.

211   MOUNT PRINCETON HOT SPRINGS
■   County Road 162   (719) 395-2361
    Nathrop, CO 81236   PR+MH

Large, modern resort between Leadvile and Salida surrounded by San Isabel National Forest. Elevation 8,500 ft. Open all year.

Natural mineral water flows out of a spring at 132º. Odorless and tasteless, this water is used in all pipes. Three outdoor swimming pools, one Olympic-size are maintained at temperatures between 85-95º, and are treated with chlorine. All pools are available to the public as well as to registered guests. There are several natural spots down in Chalk Creek. Bathing suits are required.

Locker rooms, restaurant, hotel rooms, picnic area, saddle horses, fishing and hiking are available on the premises. Skiing and river rafting are close by. A conference center/party room is available for large groups. It is five miles to all other services. Visa and MasterCard are accepted.

Directions: From US 285 in the town of Nathrop, go west five miles on CO 162 to resort.

Salida Hot Springs: This city created a major recreation center by buying a hot spring, installing a six-mile pipeline to import the geothermal water, and the building a large indoor community plunge, complete with park and playground.

212   SALIDA HOT SPRINGS
410 West Rainbow Blvd. (719) 539-6738
Salida, CO 81201   PR

Modernized, indoor municipal plunge, hot baths, park and playground. Elevation 7,000 feet. Open all year.

Natural mineral water flows out of Poncha Springs at 200º and is piped six miles to Salida. The large indoor swimming pool is maintained at a temperature of 100-104º, the lap pool is maintained at 90-92°, and a shallow baby pool at 96°. All pools are treated with chlorine. There are six private indoor soaking pools which are drained and refilled after each use and in which the water temperature is controllable by the customer. Bathing suits are required everywhere except in private soaking pools.

Locker rooms are available on the premises. It is less than five blocks to all other services. No credit cards are accepted.

Directions: From the junction of US 50 and US 285, go six miles east on US 50. Look for signs on the north side of the street.

Desert Reef Beach Club: Water temperature is regulated to correspond with the varying weather in this desert area south of Colorado Springs.

213   DESERT REEF BEACH CLUB
P.O. Box 503   **(719) 784-6134**
■ **Penrose, CO 81240**   **PR**

A small, rustic recreation area which has grown up around a geothermal well in the desert foothills south of Colorado Springs. Elevation 5,200 ft. Open all year on Wednesday, Thursday, Saturday and Sunday, 10 A.M. to 10 P.M.

Natural mineral water flows out of an artesian well at 130º and is piped to two outdoor swimming pools on a flow-through basis so that no chemical treatment of the water is necessary. Flow rate is adjusted to maintain pool temperature within a comfortable range for bathing and soaking through all seasons. The larger pool is maintained at about 100º and the smaller pool at about 105º. Bathing suits are optional.

A lawn area for picnicking and cold drinks are available on the premises. Visa and MasterCard are accepted. It is two miles to all other services. As this is a membership facility it is necessary to phone during business hours for information on guest passes, rates and directions.

This is the only modern swimming pool at *Valley View*, complete with diving board and a fun-filled game of keep away.

All of the other pools at *Valley View Hot Springs* have been excavated where one of the source springs flows from the ground, or along a nearby runoff channel.

214   VALLEY VIEW HOT SPRINGS
P.O. Box 175   (719) 256-4315
Villa Grove, CO 81155   PR+MH+CRV

Unique combination of clothing-optional primitive hot springs and primitive camping facilities, on the west slope of the Sangre De Cristo Mountains. Elevation 8,700 ft. Open all year.

Natural mineral water flows out of several springs at temperatures ranging from 85-96º. All pools are supplied on a flow-through basis so that no chemical treatment is needed. The main outdoor cement swimming pool is maintained at 90º. The outdoor soaking pool is built right over a spring, so the water flowing up through the gravel bottom maintains a temperature of 96º in the pool. The small gravel-bottom upper pool is also built right over a spring, and the pool temperature varies from 80-105º depending on the volume of snow melt. There is also a small soaking pool at 83º inside the wood-fired sauna building. The waterfall pool is maintained at 94º. Clothing is optional everywhere on the extensive grounds.

Rustic cabins and tent spaces are available on the premises. It is 12 miles to all other services. Visa and MasterCard are accepted.

Note: This is primarily a membership facility, with the premises reserved for members and their guests on holidays and weekends. The public is welcome to visit during the week. Write or phone first for full information.

Directions: From the junction of US 285 and CO 17 near Mineral Hot Springs, take the gravel road CR-GG due east seven miles to the location.

The large gravel-bottom soaking pool at *Valley View Hot Springs* maintains itself at 96º, the perfect "lolling" temperature. A cooler swimming pool tends to chill the human body, and a hotter soaking pool tends to overheat the human body, but a shallow 96º pool provides weightless comfort which can be enjoyed for hours.

This beautiful upper pool at *Valley View Hot Springs* can be reached only via a steep path, but the grand view and the magical quiet are worth the effort.

Splashland Hot Springs: At 7,500 feet, even summer days can be crisp, so a warm water pool is welcome, especially when the heat in geothermal water is free.

215 SPLASHLAND HOT SPRINGS

Box 972   (719) 589-6307(summer)
589-5772

Alamosa, CO 81101   PR

Large, rural community plunge in the center of a wide, high valley. Elevation 7,500 ft. Open Memorial Day through Labor Day.

Natural mineral water flows out of a spring at $106°$ and is piped to a large outdoor swimming pool which maintains a temperature of approximately $94°$. The water is treated with chlorine. Bathing suits are required.

Locker rooms and snack bar are available on the premises. It is one mile to a cafe, store and service station, and two miles to all other services. No credit cards are accepted.

Location: On CO 17, one mile north of town of Alamosa.

4UR Guest Ranch: The swimming pool is outdoors but the hydrojet pool is in the log building with the dressing rooms.

217   RAINBOW (WOLF CREEK PASS) HOT SPRINGS

● **Northwest of the town of Pagosa Springs**

A primitive riverside hot spring at the end of a rugged two-mile hike in the Weminuche Wilderness, northwest of CO 160. Elevation 9,000 ft. Open all year (subject to flooding).

Natural mineral water flows out of a spring at 104º and flows directly into five volunteer-built, rock-and-mud pools at the east edge of the San Juan River. A high rate of geothermal flow maintains a temperature of more than 100º in these pools. The apparent local custom is clothing optional.

There are no services available on the premises. Overnight parking is permitted at the trailhead in the Piedra Forest Service campground one mile north of US 160 on west side of the Highway 160 bridge over the Piedra River. It is 25 miles to all other services.

From US 160 on the east side of Piedra River bridge, between Pagosa Springs and Bayfield, drive north on FS 622 6.9 miles to a fork in the road. Parking area on left is signed trailhead for Sheep Creek Trail. Hike downhill on a rocky but obvious trail for about one mile to the river. Turn right and follow well-used, fairly level trail about one mile along east side of river to Coffee Creek (a clearing). Look down embankment to see volunteer built rock pools. It takes about one hour to go and one-and-one-half hours to return up the steep trail.

Source map: San Juan National Forest.

216   4UR GUEST RANCH

P.O. Box 340   (719) 658-2202
■ Creede, CO 81130   MH

Modern, deluxe, upscale guest ranch surrounded by Rio Grande National Forest. Elevation 8,400 ft. Open June 1 to September 25, by reservation only.

Natural mineral water flows out of a spring at 140º and is piped through a heat exchanger to a large hydrojet hot tub which is maintained at 105º, using no chemical treatment. The swimming pool contains cold spring water, which is heated in the heat exchanger to 78º and treated with chlorine. Bathing suits are required. Pools are for the use of registered guests only, and the minimum stay is one week, by prior reservation only.

Rooms, meals, tennis, saddle horses, fishing and hiking are available on the premises. It is four miles to all other services. Major credit cards are accepted.

Directions: From the town of South Fork on US 160, go 14 miles north on CO 149 to the village of Wagon Wheel Gap. Just 0.4 mile beyond Wagon Wheel Gap, watch for sign and turn left across bridge onto gravel road to the resort.

218A PAGOSA SPRINGS POOL (THE SPA MOTEL)

P.O. Box 37 (303) 264-5912
Pagosa Springs, CO 81147 PR+MH

Older swimming pool and bathhouse formerly reserved for motel guests, now available to the public. Located near downtown Pagosa Springs. Elevation 7,100 ft. Open all year.

Natural mineral water is pumped from a well at 130º and piped to the swimming pool and bathhouse. The outdoor swimming pool is maintained at 90º. The two indoor soaking pools, in separate men's and women's sections, are maintained at 108º. All pools have continuous flow-through so that no chemical treatment is necessary. Each of the two bathhouse sections also has its own steambath. Bathing suits are required in the outdoor pools.

Rooms, locker rooms and horse stalls are available on the premises. It is less than three blocks to all other services. Visa, American Express and MasterCard are accepted.

Directions: In Pagosa Springs on US 160, 1/2 block west of the high school, turn south across the bridge and watch for pool on your left.

▼ *Pagosa Springs Pool:* A bridge across the San Juan River connects this pool, and the nearby motel, to the center of town.

218B THE SPRING INN

P.O. Box 1799 (303) 264-4168
Pagosa Springs, CO 81147 MH+PR

Nicely refurbished inn with seven river-side mineral-water pools in downtown Pagosa Springs. Elevation 7,100 ft. Open all year.

Natural mineral water flows out of a spring at 155º and is piped to seven pools overlooking the San Juan River. One large pool holds about 20 people. The other pools range in size. All pools have continuous flow-through so that no chemical treatment is necessary. Bathing suits are required.

Rooms, massage therapy, an exercise gym is available on the premises, and fly fishing is close by. All other services are close by in town. Visa, MasterCard and American Express are accepted.

Phone for rates, reservations and directions.

▲ *The Spring Inn:* Several pools overlooking the San Juan River require no chlorination and offer a relaxing view as well.

Piedra River Hot Spring looks to be well worth the strenuous two-mile hike it takes to get there.

Just below the San Juan River people of all ages enjoy playing in the warm, gooey mud.

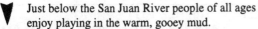

219　PIEDRA RIVER HOT SPRING

West of Pagosa Springs

A peaceful primitive spring in a beautiful mountain setting at the end of a rugged two-mile hike in the San Juan National Forest. Elevation 7,400 ft. Open all year.

Natural mineral water, at approximately 110°, flows up from the bottom of several volunteer-built, rock-and-sand pools on the east bank of the Piedra River. When necessary, evaporation cooling is supplemented by adding cold river water. The apparent local custom is clothing optional.

No services are available on the premises. It is six miles to a Forest Service campground (Lower Piedra) on FS 622, one mile north of US 160. It is 26 miles to all other services in Pagosa Springs.

Directions: From US 160, between Pagosa Springs and Bayfield, drive north on FS 622 for six miles to a fork in the road. The parking area on the left is the signed trailhead for Sheep Creek Trail. Hike up this steep trail for approximately one mile to the bridge over the river. Do not cross, but rather turn right and follow a trail up the east bank of the river for approximately one mile to Coffee Creek. Turn left toward the river to reach the springs.

Source map: San Juan National Forest (springs not shown).

59 COLORADO

▲ *Trimble Hot Springs:* These beautiful landscaped pools are the newest in the history of this century-old resort.

220 TRIMBLE HOT SPRINGS

■ 6475 County Road 203   (303)247-0111
Durango, CO 81301   PR

Restored historic resort in the scenic Animas River Valley, below the La Plata Mountains. Elevation 6,500 ft. Open all year.

Natural mineral water flows out of a spring at 111º and is piped to three outdoor pools where it is treated with ozone. The Olympic-size swimming pool is maintained at 88º, one of the hydrojet pools is maintained at 100-102º and the other is maintained at 108-110º. There are also two indoor private-space hydrojet pools in which water temperature is maintained at 102º. Bathing suits are required except in the private rooms.

Facilities include dressing rooms, a fitness studio, snack bar, picnic area and a fully-equipped apartment. Massage, physical therapy, aqua aerobics and yoga classes are available on the premises. It is two miles to a bed and breakfast inn and six miles to all other services. Visa and MasterCard are accepted.

Directions: From the city of Durango, go six miles north on US 550, then west 100 yards on Trimble Lane to springs.

▲ Different kinds of *Trimble Hot Springs* resort buildings burned down in 1892, 1931 and 1957. This new fitness studio reflects modern public interests in good health.

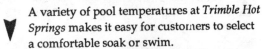 Trees, flowers, grass, and picnic tables are part of the charm of this newly-defined resort at *Trimble Hot Springs*.

A variety of pool temperatures at *Trimble Hot Springs* makes it easy for customers to select a comfortable soak or swim.

Ouray Hot Springs: This city-owned facility enjoys a large geothermal water flow and a spectacular natural setting.

221A OURAY HOT SPRINGS

P.O. Box 468   (303) 325-4638
Ouray, CO 81427   PR

Large, city-owned swimming pool and visitor information complex. Elevation 7,800 ft. Open all year.

Natural mineral water flows out of a spring at 150º and is cooled with city tap water as needed to supply three large outdoor pools. The shallow soaking pool is maintained at 100º; the deep swimming and diving pool is maintained at 80º; and the therapy pool is maintained at 105º. All pools have continuous flow-through so that no chemical treatment is needed. Bathing suits are required.

Locker rooms, snack house, fitness center and swim shop with suit rentals are available on the premises. All other services are within six blocks. Visa and MasterCard are accepted.

Location: The entire complex is easily visible on the west side of US 550 in the town of Ouray.

221B WIESBADEN HOT SPRINGS
SPA & LODGINGS   (303) 325-4347
625 5th St.
P.O. Box 349 (mailing address)
Ouray, CO 81427   PR+MH

Quaint and charming mountain resort built to complement the spectacular canyon area of Uncompahgre National Forest. Elevation 7,700 ft. Open all year.

Natural mineral water flows from three springs at temperatures ranging from 108-130º. All pools operate on a flow-through basis, requiring no chemical treatment. The outdoor swimming pool ranges from 99º to 102º . The soaking pool in the natural vapor cave is maintained at 109-110º. a challenge well worth meeting. The soaking pool in the sauna is maintained at 108º. Bathing suits are required.

A 105º flow-through soaking pool is supplied by a hot-spring waterfall in a private area called "The Lorelei." In this beautifully landscaped space, which may be rented by the hour, bathing suits are optional.

Geothermal heat is used in all buildings. Individually decorated rooms, some with fireplaces and kitchens, massage, reflexology, facials and exercise equipment are available on the premises. It is two blocks to a restaurant, store and service station, and eight blocks to overnight camping and RV hookups. Visa and MasterCard are accepted.

Location: Located on the corner of 6th Ave. and 5th St. in the town of Ouray, two blocks east of Main Street (US 550). Follow signs.

Wiesbaden Motel and Health Resort: In addition
to this controlled-temperature swimming
pool there is a vapor cave and a landscaped
area with a hot waterfall.

221C BOX CANYON LODGE AND HOT SPRINGS

45 3rd Ave.   **(303) 325-4981**
Ouray, CO 81427   **MH**

Modern lodge at the base of mountains in a quiet off-highway location adjacent to the Box Canyon Falls and the Uncompahgre River. Elevation 7,800 ft. Open all year.

Natural mineral water flows out of a spring at 140º and is piped to four continuously flow-through outdoor redwood tubs requiring no chemical treatment. The four hydrojet tubs are situated on redwood decks which are terraced up the mountainside behind the lodge, offering spectacular views of the city and surrounding mountains. Temperatures in the tubs range between 103-107º. Usage of the tubs is reserved for registered guests and bathing suits are required. Visa, MasterCard, Diners Club, American Express and Discover are accepted.

Several geothermal springs, varying in temperature from 138-156º are located on the property and the water is used to heat all lodge rooms as well as to heat shower water.

Location: Two blocks west of US 550 on 3rd Ave.

Box Canyon Lodge: Winter or summer, a soak in any one of the four outdoor tubs would feel welcome.

221D BEST WESTERN TWIN PEAKS MOTEL

125 3rd Ave.   **(303) 325-4427**
Ouray, CO 81427   **MH**

Modern, major hotel in a picturesque mountain town. Elevation 7,700 ft. Open April through October.

Natural mineral water flows out of a spring at 156º and is piped to two pools. The outdoor swimming pool is maintained at 82º; the outdoor waterfall soaking tub at 106º; and the indoor soaking pool at 104º. Pools are reserved for the use of registered guests. Bathing suits are required. Visa, MasterCard, American Express, Carte Blanche, Diners Club and Amoco are accepted.

Location: One block west of US 550 on 3rd Ave.

Best Western: After a long drive, sitting under the mineral springs waterfall in the outdoor soaking pool would do a lot to relieve a sore neck.

222 ORVIS HOT SPRINGS

■ 1585 County Rd. #3   **(303) 626-5324**
Ridgway, CO 81432   **PR+MH**

Small and charming rustic lodge with multiple geothermal pools, located in a wide mountain valley. Elevation 7,000 ft. Open all year.

Mineral water flows from several springs at temperatures ranging from 112-127º and is piped to a variety of tubs and pools, all of which operate on a flow-through basis requiring no chemical treatment. All of them are available to the public for day use as well as to registered guests.

There are four private rooms with tiled soaking pools that have a water temperature of 105-109º that are drained and cleaned every day. Immediately adjoining the sauna building there is one outside soaking pool, built of stone, which has a water temperature of 105-108º. There is one large cement indoor soaking pool (three-feet deep, 25 feet in diameter) which has a temperature of 101º in the summer and 104º in the winter. There is also one large, excavated soaking pond (six-feet deep, 30 feet in diameter) which has hot mineral water continuously flowing in from the bottom and the sides. This enlarged natural hot-spring maintains a year-round temperature of 103-105º. Clothing is optional in all pools except the 25-foot indoor soaking pool.

Facilities include six lodge rooms which share two baths. Room rates include unlimited use of sauna and pool facilities. Massage therapy available by appointment. Visa and MasterCard are accepted. It is less than two miles to the town of Ridgway and all other services. Phone for rates, hours, reservations and directions.

▲ *Orivs Hot Springs*: Very few commercial locations can offer a clothing-optional primitive soak in a hot spring pond.

▲ *Orivs* customers who prefer to avoid skinnydippers may use this indoor pool where bathing suits are required.

65 COLORADO

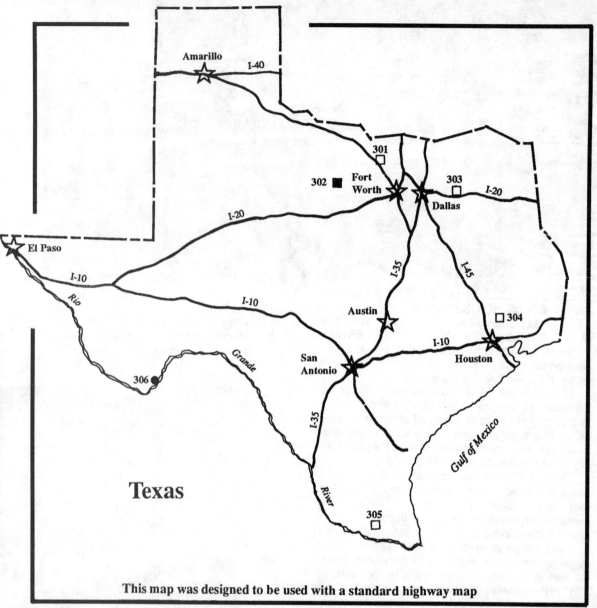

Amarillo

I-40

301

302 ■ Fort
Worth

303

I-20

Dallas

I-20

El Paso

I-10

Rio

I-35

I-45

I-10

Austin

☐ 304

I-10

Grande

San
Antonio

Houston

306 ●

I-35

Texas

River

305

This map was designed to be used with a standard highway map

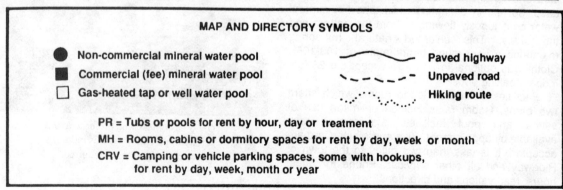

MAP AND DIRECTORY SYMBOLS

● Non-commercial mineral water pool

■ Commercial (fee) mineral water pool

☐ Gas-heated tap or well water pool

〜〜〜 Paved highway

– – – Unpaved road

⋯⋯ Hiking route

PR = Tubs or pools for rent by hour, day or treatment

MH = Rooms, cabins or dormitory spaces for rent by day, week or month

CRV = Camping or vehicle parking spaces, some with hookups,
        for rent by day, week, month or year

301 BLUEBONNET

☐ Rt. 1, Box 146   (817) 627-2313
Alvord, TX 76225   PR+MH+CRV

Modern nudist resort on 66 acres of rolling hills, four miles north of Decatur in northern Texas. Elevation 1100 ft. Open all year.

The indoor whirlpool spa is filled with gas-heated well water, treated with chlorine, and maintained at 103º. The outdoor swimming pool, surrounded by two large sundecks, is filled with solar-heated well water, treated with chlorine, and maintained at 80º. Clothing is prohibited in spa, pool and sauna; optional elsewhere.

Facilities include cabins, trailers, tenting spaces, RV hook-ups, tenting spaces, clubhouse, sauna, and volleyball, tennis and shuffleboard courts. Visa, MasterCard and American Express are accepted. It is four miles to all other services.

Note: This is a membership organization not open to the public for drop-in visits, but interested visitors may be issued a guest pass by prior arrangement. Telephone or write for information and directions.

302 STOVALL HOT WELLS

■ PO Box 68   (817) 362-4423
South Bend, TX 76081   PR+MH+CRV

A healing-oriented residential resort in northern Texas which combines mineral water therapy with energy balancing and other therapies. Elevation 500 ft. Open all year.

Natural mineral water flows out of a well at 130º and is piped to separate men's and women's bathhouses, each containing two large bathing pools. Pool water temperatures are maintained at 101º on a continuous flow-through basis so no chemical treatment of the water is necessary. Bathing suits are not required in bathhouses. Day-use customers are welcome.

Facilities include guest rooms, cabins and spaces for campers and RV's. Reflexology, acupressure, mineral-water therapy, massage and energy-balancing are available on the premises. No credit cards are accepted. It is 12 miles to a store, restaurant, service station and other services.

Phone for rates, reservations and directions.

303 PONDAROSA RANCH

☐ P.O. Box 133   (903) 873-3311
Wills Point, TX 75169   PR+MH+CRV

Modern, residential nature park and health resort on 60 rolling acres, 55 miles east of Dallas. Elevation 2,000 ft. Open all year.

The outdoor hydrospa is filled with gas-heated well and tap water, treated with chlorine, and is maintained at 102º. The outdoor swimming pool is filled with unheated well and tap water and treated with chlorine. Clothing is prohibited in the spa, pool and sauna; optional elsewhere.

Other facilities include rental trailers, RV hook-ups, tenting spaces, a clubhouse, and volleyball, horseshoe and shuffleboard courts, plus a full service restaurant during the summer season. Visa and MasterCard are accepted. It is eight miles to all other services.

Note: This is a membership organization, but it is open to the public for drop-in visits. No reservations are required except for the rental trailers. Telephone or write for further information.

304 LIVE OAK RESORT, INC.

☐ Rt. 1, Box 916   (409) 878-2216
Washington, TX 77880   PR+MH+CRV

A well-maintained, family nudist park with 17 acres of mowed lawn, interspersed with shade-providing oak trees, nestled in rolling farm country near Houston. Elevation 525 ft. Open all year.

Gas-heated well water, chlorine-treated, is used in an outdoor hydropool maintained at 104º. The Olympic-size swimming pool using similar water is unheated but averages over 80º between June and September. Clothing is optional on the first visit, except in the pools, where it is prohibited at all times.

Cabins, a full-service restaurant, camping and RV hookups are available on the premises. Other facilities include a lighted, sand volleyball court and a clubhouse with pool table and ping pong. A children's playground with a waterslide is also available. It is four miles to a store and service station. No credit cards are accepted.

Note: This is a membership organization not open to the public for drop-in visits, but a guest pass may be issued by prior arrangement. Resort rules prohibit guns, drugs and erotic behavior. Phone for more information and directions.

Sandpipers Holiday Park: The unheated water must feel refreshing in the hot Texas summer sun.

305 SANDPIPERS HOLIDAY PARK

☐ Rte. 7, Box 309   (210) 383-7589
Edinburg, TX 78539   PR+MH+CRV

North America's southernmost nudist park located on 21 acres, seven miles north of Edinburg and 20 miles north of Mexico. Elevation 100 ft. Open all year.

The outdoor hydrojet spa is filled with gas-heated well water, treated with chlorine, and maintained at 103º. The outdoor Olympic-size swimming pool is filled with unheated well water in the summer and is gas-heated in the winter to maintain 85º. Clothing is prohibited in the spa and pool, optional elsewhere.

Facilities include rental units, tenting spaces, RV hook-ups, clubhouse, volleyball and shuffleboard courts and two lighted tennis courts. Meals are served on weekends. Visa and MasterCard are accepted. It is one mile to all other services.

Note: This is a membership organization not open to the public for drop-in visits, but prospective members and guests may be issued a guest pass by prior arrangement. Telephone or write for information.

306 BOQUILLAS (LANGFORD) HOT SPRING

● **Near the town of Lajitas, Texas**

Historic masonry hot pool in the ruins of an old resort on the banks of the Rio Grande River. Located near the Rio Grande Village Campground in Big Bend National Park. Elevation 1,800 ft. Open all year.

Natural mineral water flows out of the ground at 105º into a large, shallow soaking pool a few feet above river level. Bathing suits are advisable in the daytime.

There are no services on the premises. It is six miles to a store, service station, overnight camping and RV hookups, 28 miles to a motel and restaurant.

Directions: From Big Bend National Park Headquarters, drive 16 miles toward Rio Grand Village Campground. Turn right at Hot Springs sign, then drive two miles on dirt road to the end and walk 1/4 mile downriver to hot spring.

Source map: *Big Bend National Park.*

Boquillas Hot Spring: Geothermal water collects into a soaking pool behind the foundation blocks of an historic resort building, long ago swept away by floods.

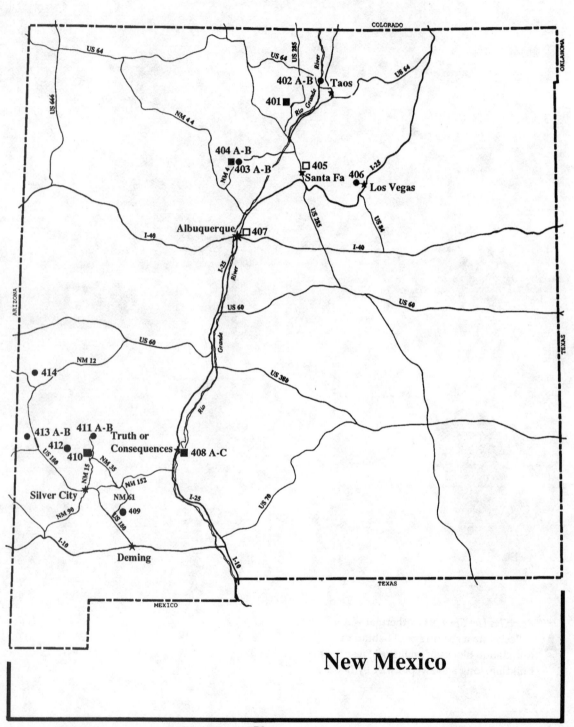

This map was designed to be used with a standard highway map

New Mexico

401   OJO CALIENTE RESORT

Box 468   (505) 583-2233
■ Ojo Caliente, NM   PR+MH+CRV

An older resort and bathhouse located in the foothills of Carson National Forest, 46 miles north of Santa Fe. Elevation 6,300 ft. Open all year.

Natural mineral water flows out of five different springs with different temperatures and different mineral contents. There are separate men's and women's bathhouses, each containing a large soaking pool at 113° and individual tubs with temperatures up to 105°. There are also coed soaking tubs and a year-round swimming pool maintained at a temperature of 80°.

Massage, sweat wrap, herbal facials, dining room, lodging, and RV hookups, are available on the premises. Visa and MasterCard are accepted. It is 25 miles to a public bus, and pick-up service is available for registered guests. Phone for details.

Directions: From Santa Fe, go 46 miles north on US 285. Watch for signs.

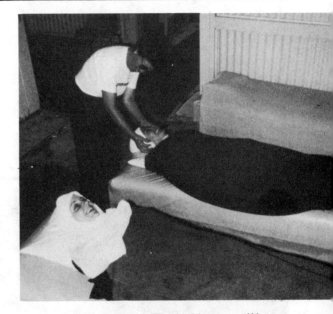

Ojo Caliente Resort: The bathhouse staff keeps customers comfortable while they are tightly wound in a traditional sweat wrap.

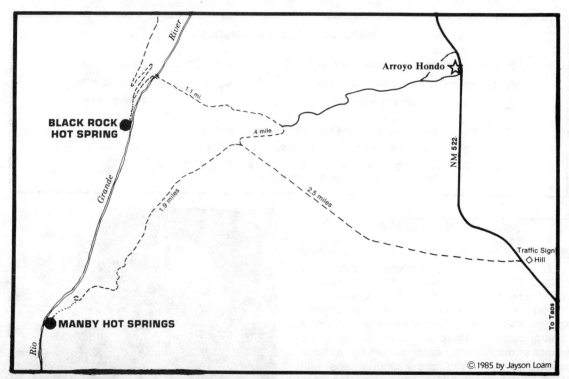

BLACK ROCK HOT SPRING

Arroyo Hondo

NM 522

1.1 mi.

.4 mile

1.9 miles

2.5 miles

Traffic Sign
◇ Hill

To Taos

Rio Grande River

MANBY HOT SPRINGS

© 1985 by Jayson Loam

72

Black Rock Hot Springs: The jagged rocks look somewhat forbidding, but this crystal clear pool has a lovely soft sand bottom.

402A   BLACK ROCK HOT SPRINGS
(see map)
● **West of the town of Arroyo Hondo**

Rugged, but friendly, sand-bottom rock pool located on the west bank of the Rio Grande Gorge, just a few feet above river level. Elevation 6,500 ft. Open all year, subject to flooding.

Natural mineral water flows up through the bottom at a rate sufficient to maintain pool temperature at 97° except when high water in the river floods the pool. The apparent local custom is clothing optional.

There are no services available. It is three miles to a store, cafe, service station, etc., and nine miles to RV hookups. Note: Unpaved roads may become impassable during wet weather.

Directions: There is a small parking area at the end of the first switchback on the gravel road that winds up the west face of the gorge. Follow the trail downstream from that parking area.

402B   MANBY HOT SPRINGS   (see map)
● **Southwest of the town of Arroyo Hondo**

Two primitive soaking pools in the ruins of an old stagecoach stop on the east bank of the Rio Grande Gorge. Elevation 6,500 ft. Open all year.

Natural mineral water flows out of the ground at 97° directly into two rock pools large enough for five or six people. The lower pool is only slightly above low water in the river, so the temperature depends on the amount of cold water seeping into the volunteer-built rock pool. The apparent local custom is clothing optional.

There are no services on the premises. There is a limited amount of nearby level space in which overnight parking is not prohibited. It is four miles to a store, cafe, service station, etc., and ten miles to RV hookups. Note: Unpaved roads may become impassable during wet weather.

Directions: Drive southwest from Arroyo Hondo to the parking area at the end of the gravel road, then hike down the grade of the old stagecoach road to the springs.

Source maps: USGS *Arroyo Hondo*.

Manby Hot Springs: For those who like to alternate relaxing hot water soaks with invigorating dips in cold river water, this is the convenient place for both.

North of the town of Jemez Springs

A unique, sand-bottom pool on a steep hillside with a spectacular view of surrounding mountains. Located in the Santa Fe National Forest on the east side of the Jemez River. Elevation 6,000 ft. Open all year.

Natural mineral water (106°) flows up through the sandy bottom into a rock-bordered pool large enough for ten people. The rate of flow-through is enough to keep the pool clean and averaging 104°. Several years ago the spring had a posted Forest Service rule requiring bathing suits on Thursday, Friday and Saturday, with suits optional on Sunday, Monday, Tuesday and Wednesday. Now the apparent local custom is clothing optional every day.

There are no services available. It is 1.5 miles north of the parking area to a store, gas, restaurant and lodge in La Cueva, at the intersection of NM 4 and NM 126, five miles to a campground, seven miles to an AYH youth hostel and 17 miles to RV hookups.

Directions: From the town of Jemez Springs, go seven miles north on NM 4 to a large parking area on the east side of the highway. This is two miles past "Battleship Picnic Area." From the town of Los Alamos, drive west on NM 501 to the intersection in La Cueva with NM 126 and NM 4. Then go south on NM 4 for 1.5 miles to the large parking area on the east side of the road. The short trail from the parking area includes a log spanning the Jemez River and a steep slope up to the springs. During snow and rain the slope can become very slippery.

Source map: *Santa Fe National Forest*.

◀ *Spence Hot Springs:* This spot has a lovely
  forest view and is so relaxing that students
▼ can even do homework while sunbathing
  between soaks in the pool.

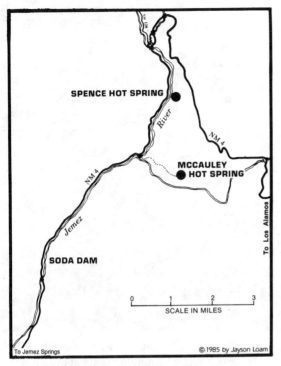

McCauley Hot Spring: The retaining dam which holds this pool has lasted more than 50 years since it was built by the CCC.

403B   MCCAULEY HOT SPRING (see map)

North of the town of Jemez Springs

Very large, warm pool in a gorgeous mountain clearing. Elevation 7,300 ft. Open approximately mid-April through October.

Natural mineral water flows out of the ground at 90° directly into a two-foot-deep pond, 40 feet in diameter. The rate of flow is sufficient to hold the temperature at approximately 85°. The apparent local custom is clothing optional.

There are no services on the premises. However, the guppies and neon tetras that live in the pool will entertain you by nibbling on your body hair. It is 3.5 miles to a store, gas, restaurant and lodge in La Cueva, at the intersection of NM 4 and NM 126, five miles to a campground and AYH youth hostel, and 17 miles to RV hookups.

Directions: From Jemez Springs, go 5.2 miles north on NM 4 to Battleship Rock picnic area. From Los Alamos, drive west on NM 501 to La Cueva, turn left (south) on NM 4 for 3.5 miles to the Battleship Picnic Area. Starting from the firepit gazebo in the picnic area, hike 1 1/4 miles up USFS trail 137 to spring and campsite. This trail is moderately strenuous, especially at this altitude.

75 NEW MEXICO

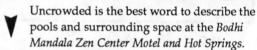

Bodhi Mandala Zen Center Motel and Hot Springs: Geothermal steam and snow-clad mountains are fit subjects for meditation.

Uncrowded is the best word to describe the pools and surrounding space at the *Bodhi Mandala Zen Center Motel and Hot Springs.*

404A BODHI MANDALA ZEN CENTER MOTEL AND HOT SPRINGS
Box 8 (505) 829-3854
Jemez Springs, NM 87205 MH

A four-unit motel with primitive, riverbank hot pools, operated by the Bodhi Mandala Zen Center. Located in the town of Jemez Springs. Elevation 6,200 ft. Open all year, subject to weather conditions and special events at the center.

Natural mineral water flows out of the ground at 169°, then into four rock-and-sand soaking pools where natural cooling results in varying temperatures. Bathing suits are required. Phone ahead for current information. Pools are reserved for motel guests only. No drop-ins, please.

It is one block to a store, cafe and seven miles to a service station. Phone for rates, reservations and directions.

During the winter months it is comforting to know that your warm motel room is only a few steps away when you leave the hot pool at the *Bodhi Mandala Zen Center.*

404B JEMEZ SPRINGS BATH HOUSE
Box 105 (505) 829-3303
Jemez Springs, NM 87205 PR

An older, traditional bathhouse located on the main street, operated by the city of Jemez Springs. Elevation 6,200 ft. Open all year.

Natural mineral water flows out of a city-owned springs at 169° and is piped to a cooling tank and then to the bathhouse. There are eight private rooms, each containing a one-person bathtub and a private outdoor redwood tub available to groups of up to six. Cool and hot mineral water are mixed to provide the desired water temperature. Tubs are drained and refilled after each use, so no chemical treatment of the water is necessary. Clothing is optional.

Massage and reflexology and a fully equipped fitness room are available on the premise, as is a store selling local crafts, beauty supplies, cold drinks and pastries. Visa and MasterCard are accepted. It is one block to a store, restaurants and service station. Phone for rates, reservations and directions.

Jemez Springs Bath House: Colorful curtains, a fitness room and a small cafe are all part of an upgrade on this older, traditional spa.

405 TEN THOUSAND WAVES

P.O. Box 10103   (505) 988-1047
(Reservations) (505) 982-9304
☐   Santa Fe, NM 87504   PR

An intriguing blend of American technology and Japanese hot-tub traditions, located on Ski Basin Rd., northeast of Santa Fe.

Ten pools in private enclosures are for rent to the public. One pool is roofed in, a sauna is available in three of the enclosures, and a steam room is in another. A communal wood tub and sauna, large enough for 25 people, and a separate women's tub are also available. The pools use gas-heated well water treated with ultraviolet light and hydrogen peroxide and are maintained at 104-106°. Bathing suits are optional everywhere, except at the front desk.

Kimonos, sandals, shampoo and hair dryers are provided. Private lockers are available in the men's and women's dressing rooms. Massage, herbal wraps, salt glows, watsu in-water massage, East Indian cleansing treatments, facials and a juice bar are available on the premises. Visa, MasterCard and Discover Card are accepted. Phone for rates, reservations and directions.

▲ *Montezuma Hot Springs*: Volunteers have built and maintain several soaking pools near the various springs.

406 MONTEZUMA HOT SPRINGS

●   **Northwest of the town of Las Vegas (NM)**

The once-abandoned ruins of a major turn-of-the-century hot-springs resort bathhouse. Located at the mouth of a mountain canyon, just across the Gallinas River from the lavish Victorian "Montezuma's Castle." Elevation 6450 ft. Open all year.

Natural mineral water flows out of several springs (94-113°) into eight outdoor old-fashioned cement soaking pits of various sizes and depths up to six feet, resulting in a wide range of temperature choices. Continuous flow-through (15 gallons per minute) eliminates the need for chemical treatment of the water. Volunteers are fastidious about keeping the pools clean, draining and scrubbing them when algae collect. Bathing suits are required.

There are no services available on the premises. It is six miles to a store, cafe, service station, etc.

Directions: From the town of Las Vegas, go six miles northwest on NM 65. Two signs along the right side of the road indicate "Hot Springs Baths," although the stone bathhouse with five indoor pools is now fenced and closed. The outdoor pools are still open to the public, 24 hours per day, year-round, at no charge.

▲ The use of wood and greenery creates a degree of primitive atmosphere around the private-space pools at *Ten Thousand Waves*.

407 SPLASH
9800 Montgomery NE, Ste. S
(505) 293-3008
☐ Albuquerque, NM 87111 PR

Modern, suburban rent-a-tub facility located in a commercial corner building north of downtown Albuquerque.

Private-space hot pools using gas-heated tap water treated with bromine are for rent to the public. There are fifteen indoor acrylic hydropools with water temperature maintained at 103-105° Each room also contains a shower and private dressing area. Children under 12 are free when accompanied by parents.

Massage is available by appointment. Visa and MasterCard are accepted. Phone for rates, reservations and directions.

Splash: The design of modern rent-a-tub spaces incorporates a large amount of tile because it is so easy to keep clean.

THE SPRINGS OF TRUTH OR CONSEQUENCES

There are three natural mineral water establishments located in the hot springs area of Truth or Consequences. All of them have their own flowing geothermal source pools and pipe the hot water to various indoor pools as needed.

The city is located on the Rio Grande River below Elephant Butte Dam. Elevation 4,300 ft. Open all year. A cafe, store, service station and RV hookups are within four blocks of every location.

408A ARTESIAN BATH HOUSE AND TRAILER PARK
312 Marr (505) 894-2684
■ Truth or Consequences, NM 87901 PR+CRV

Older bathhouse and RV park.

Eight private rooms, each containing a padded sweating bench and ceramic tile tub, filled with fresh mineral water for each customer. Five are single-size and three are double-size tubs. Water temperature is uncontrollable up to 112°.

RV hookups are available on the premises. No credit cards are accepted.

408B CHARLES MOTEL AND BATH HOUSE
701 Broadway (505) 894-7154
■ Truth or Consequences, NM 87901
PR+MH

Older bathhouse and motel with some new units.

Separate indoor men's and women's sections, each equipped with a sauna, steambath and four individual tubs with controllable water temperature up to 110°.

Massage is available on the premises. Visa and MasterCard are accepted.

408C MARSHALL APARTMENTS AND BATHS
311 Marr (505) 894-9286
■ Truth or Consequences, NM 87901
PR+MH

Older bathhouse and motel units converted to apartments, now rented by the week or month.

Four private rooms with large pools, each with a gravel bottom and direct flow-through of unchlorinated hot mineral water. Temperatures range from 106-112°.

Massage available on the premises. No credit cards are accepted.

79 NEW MEXICO

Welcome back to *Faywood Hot Springs*. It has recently been purchased by a family who are in the process of rebuilding cabins, an RV park and a cafe. The pools are open at this time and a soak, summer or winter, (often surrounded by snow), is a real treat. It's encouraging to see a hot spring reopen.

---

409   FAYWOOD HOT SPRINGS
165 Highway 61   (505) 536-9663
HC 71 Box 1240
Faywood, NM 88034   PR

Located halfway between Deming and Silver City, next to the City of Rocks State Park, are the remains of a once elaborate resort. Recently purchased, the springs are in the process of being renovated and developed. Elevation 5,000 ft. Open all year.

Natural mineral water flows from the top of a tufa dome at 130° downhill into several stone soaking pools in a naturally beautiful desert setting. There are both clothing-only and clothing-optional areas.

A true desert oasis, with large trees and park-like surroundings, Faywood offers several soaking pools, picnic tables and walking trails. Cabins, an RV park and a cafe are planned for the near future. (Phone for the status of construction.) It is 15 miles to a store, and 1 mile to RV and overnight camping.

Directions: From Deming take 180 north 24 miles, turn right (east) on Highway 61, and go about 2 miles from the intersection of 180 and 61. From Silver City take 180 south about 25 miles, turn left on Highway 61, and proceed about 2 miles from the intersection.

410 GILA HOT SPRINGS VACATION CENTER (see map)

Gila Hot Springs, Rte. 11 (505) 534-9551
Silver City, NM 88061   MH+CRV

An all-year vacation resort located in the middle of the Gila National Forest. Elevation 5,000 ft. Open all year

Natural mineral water flows from an artesian well at 160° and is piped across the Gila River to the Vacation Center where it is used in an enclosed tile hydropool, available only to registered guests. Pool water temperature is maintained at 90° in summer and 100° in winter. Clothing is optional within the enclosure.

Also, natural mineral water at 150°, flowing from the springs on the east bank of the Gila River, is piped to the riverside camping area. Registered guests can use this hot water to make warm pools along the edge of the river. Bathing suits are required.

The hot water from both the artesian well and the springs are used for drinking.

Store, snack bar, service station, laundromat, showers, light housekeeping apartments, trailer rentals, RV hookups, campground and picnic areas are available on the premises. Credit cards are accepted only at the store.

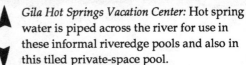

Gila Hot Springs Vacation Center: Hot spring water is piped across the river for use in these informal riveredge pools and also in this tiled private-space pool.

411A LIGHTFEATHER (MIDDLE FORK) HOT SPRING

● (see map)
North of the Gila Visitors Center

A primitive, rock-and-sand soaking pool on the Middle Fork of the Gila River, one-half mile from the Gila Visitors Center. Elevation 5,800 ft. Open all year, subject to high water in the river, which must be forded twice.

Natural mineral water flows out of the spring at 150° directly into a large rock-and-sand pool where the water gradually cools as it flows to the other end. Bathing suits are probably advisable during the daytime at this location.

There are no services available. It is two miles to a store, cafe, service station and RV hookups.

Directions: Allow two hours for the 44 mile drive from Silver City along scenic route NM 15, a two-lane mountain road which twists and winds through the Gila National Forest.

◀ *Lightfeather Hot Spring:* The source spring in the foreground emits 150º water which tends to float on top, so the pool must be occasionally stirred to avoid a scalding.

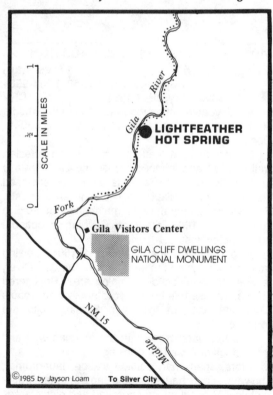

SCALE IN MILES

Gila River

● **LIGHTFEATHER HOT SPRING**

Fork

● **Gila Visitors Center**

GILA CLIFF DWELLINGS NATIONAL MONUMENT

NM 15

Middle

©1985 by Jayson Loam   **To Silver City**

411B HOUSE LOG CANYON HOT SPRINGS

● **Northwest of the Gila Visitors Center**

Remote unimproved hot springs on a tree- and fern-covered hillside in the Gila Wilderness, where the canyon meets the Middle Fork of the Gila River. (The Gila Visitors Center information incorrectly places the springs at Jordan Canyon and refers to them as "Jordan Springs") Elevation 6,200 ft. Accessible only during low water level in the river.

Natural mineral water flows out of several springs at 92° and cascades directly into a log- and rock-dammed pool large enough to hold ten people. The apparent local custom is clothing optional.

There are no services available. The 9.5 mile hike from the Visitors Center requires fording the river 45 times.

A mile farther up the Middle Fork, beyond Big Bear Canyon, are more warm springs called THE MEADOWS, at the mouth of Indian Creek Canyon.

Note: A wilderness permit is required before entering this area. While obtaining your permit from the ranger at the Gila Visitors Center, check on the adequacy of your provisions and on the level of the water in the river.

Source maps: Gila National Forest. USGS *Woodland Park.* (Note: These hot springs are not shown on either map.)

An excellent coated topographical map of the area is available from the Gila Visitors Center for a nominal fee. Purchase a copy, take it to the Gila Hot Springs Vacation Center (one mile south) and discuss your plans with the store owners, who have hiked in the canyon area for years. Supplies can also be obtained at the store for whatever hiking trip you choose.

▲ *House Log Canyon Hot Springs:* This soaking pool is in a lush natural setting, and so is the hike, which is where you will spend most of your time. Enjoy the trip, too.

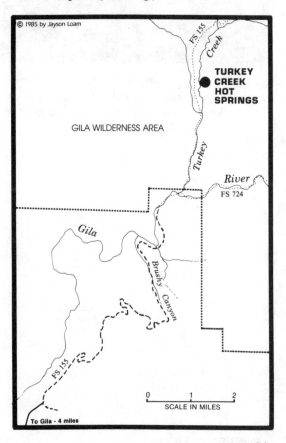

Turkey Creek Hot Springs: Experienced soakers can fine tune the temperature in each pool by moving just a few rocks.

© 1985 by Jayson Loam

FS 155

Creek

TURKEY
CREEK
HOT
SPRINGS

GILA WILDERNESS AREA

Turkey

River

FS 724

Gila

Brushy Canyon

FS 155

0   1   2
SCALE IN MILES

To Gila - 4 miles

412   TURKEY CREEK HOT SPRINGS
(see map)
North of the town of Gila

Several truly primitive hot springs accessible only via a challenging and rewarding hike into the Gila Wilderness. Elevation 5,200 ft. Not accessible during high water flow in the Gila River.

Natural mineral water (approximately 160°) flows out of many rock fractures along the bottom of Turkey Creek Canyon and combines with creek water in several volunteer-built soaking pools. Temperatures are regulated by controlling the relative amounts of hot and cold water entering a pool. The apparent local custom is clothing optional.

There are no services available, but there are a limited number of overnight camping spots near the hot springs. Visitors have done an excellent job of packing out all their trash; please do your part to maintain this tradition. All services are 17 miles away.

Directions: From the end of the jeep road, Wilderness Trail FS 724 crosses the Gila River several times before reaching a junction with Wilderness Trail FS 155, which starts up Turkey Creek Canyon. Approximately two miles from that junction, FS 155 begins to climb up onto a ridge separating Turkey Creek from Skeleton Canyon. Do not follow FS 155 up onto that ridge. Instead, stay in the bottom of Turkey Creek Canyon, even though there is often no visible trail. Another half-mile will bring you to the first of the springs.

Source maps: Gila National Forest. Gila Wilderness and Black Range Primitive Area. USGS *Canyon Hill*. (Note: Turkey Creek Hot Springs does not appear on any of these maps.)

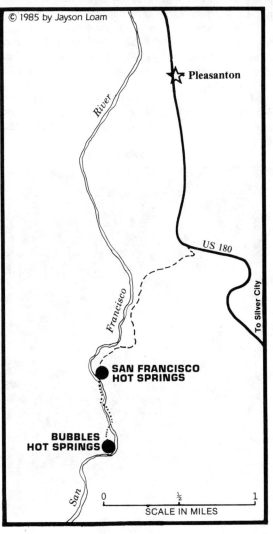

© 1985 by Jayson Loam

Pleasanton

River

US 180

Francisco

To Silver City

**SAN FRANCISCO
HOT SPRINGS**

**BUBBLES
HOT SPRINGS**

San

0   ½   1

SCALE IN MILES

▲ *San Francisco Hot Springs:* These pools are washed away every year when heavy run-off changes the banks of the Gila River.

413A   SAN FRANCISCO HOT SPRINGS
(see map)

● **South of the town of Pleasanton**

Several primitive hot springs along the east bank of the San Francisco River in the Gila National Forest. Elevation 4,600 ft. Open all year.

Natural mineral water flows out of the ground at 110° into a series of volunteer-built rock-and-mud riverbank pools. The parking area for this popular site is only ten yards away, so the Forest Service has posted a "nudity prohibited" sign, but clothing optional seems to be the local custom when there are no rangers around.

There are no services available. Primitive camping is permitted for up to seven days on the river side of the parking area which is Forest Service land. Overnight camping is not permitted on the inland side under the trees, which is private property. Campers have done an excellent job of respecting the pristine beauty of the area and packing out trash. There is also Forest Service trash collection once per week. It is five miles to a store, cafe and service station, and 12 miles to RV hookups.

Directions: Watch for San Francisco Hot Spring signs on US 180, two miles south of Pleasanton. When approaching from the south, the signs will be on the left, 1.1 miles after crossing the Dugway Canyon bridge. Turn off onto the gravel road which leads to the parking area. This road crosses two creek beds and can be muddy after rain or snow.

85 NEW MEXICO

413B BUBBLES HOT SPRINGS
●   **(see map on preceding page)**
South of the town of Pleasanton

One of the truly great unimproved hot springs in terms of size, water temperature, location and scenery. Elevation 4,600 ft. Open all year, except during high water in the river.

Several years ago a major flood scoured out a 50- by 100-foot pool under a spectacular cliff, deposited a giant sand bar in front of the pool, and dropped the normal river flow into a channel 100 yards away. Natural mineral water now flows up through the sandy pool bottom at 106°, maintaining the entire five-foot-deep pool at 96-102°, depending on air temperature. The pool even skims and cleans itself by flowing out over a small volunteer-built dam. Other nearby geothermal water outflows feed a series of small volunteer-built pools which maintain a temperature of 106°. The apparent local custom is clothing optional.

There are no services available, although primitive tent camping is permitted for up to seven days on the flat area near the pool. It is five miles to a store, cafe and service station, and 12 miles to RV hookups.

Directions: From the parking area at San Francisco Hot Springs, hike downstream approximately 1/2 mile, crossing the river three times.

Source map: USGS *Wilson Mountain*.

Bubbles Hot Springs: Volunteers have excavated shallow soaking pools in the source springs which feed the main pool under the cliff in the background.

The main pool at *Bubbles Hot Springs* skims itself as it overflows toward the river.

414   FRISCO BOX HOT SPRING

● **East of the town of Luna**

Shallow, concrete soaking pool in a scenic canyon at the end of a rough road and a rugged but beautiful 1 1/2 mile trail. Elevation 6,800 ft. Open all year.

Natural mineral water flows out of a spring at 100° and is piped to a 4-foot by 8-foot by 20-inch deep concrete box. The apparent local custom is clothing optional.

There are no services available on the premises. There is a walk-in camping area just north across the river from the hot spring. Overnight parking is permitted on level land just east of the private property gate. It is ten miles to groceries and gasoline, and 20 miles to all other services.

Directions: Start at the Luna Ranger Station to obtain current information on weather conditions, river level and a Gila National Forest Map. From US 180 in Luna drive north on FS 19 (signed *Bill Knight Gap Road*) and turn east on FS 210 (signed *Frisco Box Road*) to a private-property gate. Pass through the gate, carefully closing it after you, and continue east until road becomes impassable. Park and hike an additional 1 1/2 miles east, fording the river six times. On the south bank look for a pipe and sign *Frisco Box Spring*. Follow a well worn, slightly uphill path 75 yards to the concrete box. Enjoy the spectacular view of the river and surrounding mountains.

▲ The main pool at *Bubbles Hot Springs* was formed when this entire corner under a high cliff was scoured out by the Gila River during a record-setting flood.

This map was designed to be used with a standard highway map

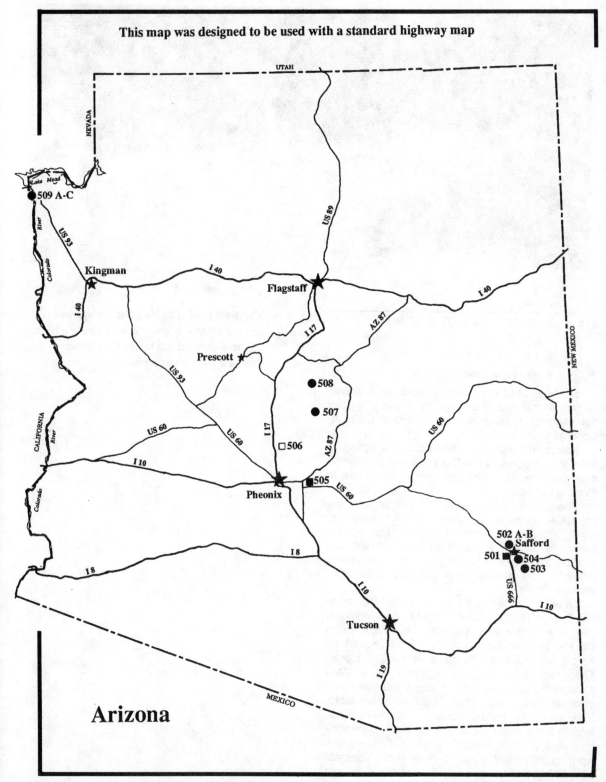

● Non-commercial mineral water pool

◼ Commercial (fee) mineral water pool

▢ Gas-heated tap or well water pool

〜〜〜 Paved highway

- - - - - Unpaved road

⋯⋯⋯ Hiking route

PR = Tubs or pools for rent by hour, day or treatment

MH = Rooms, cabins or dormitory spaces for rent by day, week or month

CRV = Camping or vehicle parking spaces, some with hookups, for rent by day, week, month or year

501 KACHINA MINERAL SPRINGS SPA

Route 2, Box 987   (602) 428-7212
◼ Safford, AZ 85546   PR

Therapy-oriented bathhouse located in the suburbs south of Safford. Elevation 3,000 ft. Open all year.

Natural mineral water flows out of an artesian well at 108º and is piped into private-room soaking tubs. There are six large, tiled sunken tubs. They are drained, cleaned and refilled after each customer so that no chemical treatment is necessary. A free hot-pool soak comes with each therapy service, but private-pool use may also be rented. No credit cards are accepted. Phone for rates and reservations.

Directions: From the intersection of US 70 and US 666 in Safford, go six miles south on US 666, then turn right on Cactus Rd. for 1/4 mile.

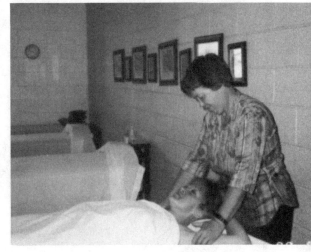

▲ *Kachina Mineral Springs Spa:* Mrs. Lilly gives her careful personal attention to each physical therapy customer.

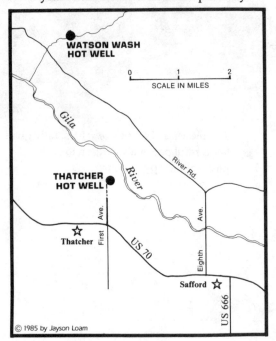

Watson Wash Hot Well: Volunteers don't build a fancy soaking pool because each year's flash floods would sweep it away.

WATSON WASH HOT WELL

THATCHER HOT WELL

Gila River

River Rd

First Ave.

Eighth Ave.

☆ Thatcher

US 70

Safford ☆

US 666

0   1   2
SCALE IN MILES

© 1985 by Jayson Loam

502A   WATSON WASH HOT WELL
(see map)

Near the town of Safford

A delightful little sand-bottom pool surrounded by willows in a primitive setting. This is also a favorite party spot for local youths, so it may be slightly tainted with broken bottles and other party trash. Elevation 3,000 ft. Open all year, subject to flash floods.

Natural mineral water flows out of a well casing at 102º and directly into a volunteer-built, shallow pool large enough for three or four people directly under the outflow spout. The surrounding pool is shallow and considerably cooler. Clothing optional is the apparent local custom at this remote location.

There are no services available on the premises. On the plateau above the wash there is unlimited level space on which overnight parking is not prohibited. It is six miles to a store, cafe, service station and other services.

Directions: From US 70 in Safford, go north on Eighth Ave. across the river to the highway "Y." Bear left on Safford-Bryce Road. At 4.3 miles from "Y" intersection, Safford-Bryce Road dips down into a dry wash. Turn right directly into the wash. Most portions are rough gravel, with some areas of hard packed earth and a few sandy spots, all of which are passable in a standard passenger vehicle, except during or just after heavy rains. This is the access route taken by most locals who come to Watson Wash to soak and party. At 0.5 miles you will see the pool on the left, surrounded by trees.

502B   THATCHER HOT WELL   (see map)

● **Near the town of Thatcher**

A substantial flow of hot mineral water out of a riverbank well on the edge of a small town. Elevation 2,900 ft. Open all year, subject to flash floods.

Natural mineral water flows out of a large well casing at 112º, then runs across mud flats toward the current channel occupied by the Gila River. Volunteers dig shallow soaking pools in the mud adjoining the flow of 112º water, controlling the pool water temperature by limiting the amount of hot water admitted. Bring your own shovel; the volunteer-built pools are very temporary. It is possible to drive within five yards of the hot well, so bathing suits are advisable in the daytime.

There are no services available on the premises. There is a limited amount of adjoining space on which overnight parking is not prohibited. It is one mile to a store, cafe, service station and other services.

Directions: From US 70 in Thatcher, drive north on First Avenue for 0.6 mile to the end of the pavement. Continue on the hard packed dirt road to the river bed and the hot well.

 Thatcher Hot Well: Yearly floods are also the reason no one builds a fancy soaking pool on these Gila River mud flats.

 Mineral water flows faster from the large *Thatcher Hot Well* casing than from many natural crack-in-the-rock hot springs.

Hot Well Dunes: When pointed straight up the well outflow pipe delivers a solid 200-gallons-per-minute shower bath.

503   HOT WELL DUNES

● **Southeast of Safford**

A large cement soaking tub surrounded by hundreds of acres of Bureau of Land Management (BLM) desert sand dunes popular with drivers of off-road-vehicles. Elevation 3,450 ft. Open all year, subject to flash floods.

Geothermal mineral water flows out of an artesian well at the rate of 200 gallons per minute and a temperature of 106º. A swivel pipe conducts the water into a converted cement septic tank which volunteers have mounted on cinder blocks. Periodic draining and cleaning of this ingenious soaking pool is also provided by volunteers. Overflow from the tub spills into an adjoining shallow sand-bottom pool which provides soaking at a lower water temperature. Bathing suits are recommended on busy holidays and weekends, but the apparent local custom on other days is clothing optional.

There are no facilities on the premises but up to two weeks of camping is permitted anywhere on the level ground in this desert area. You will need to bring all your own supplies including water, but the BLM does provide trash bins which are emptied several times per week. It is 32 miles to all services in Safford.

There are several access roads to the area but only the following one is recommended for standard passenger vehicles: From Safford follow US 70 east for seven miles to the Agricultural Inspection Station for vehicles entering from New Mexico. A 0.3 miles east of the station turn right (south) onto an unmarked gravel road. Continue south for 25.4 miles on this hard-surface gravel road which is wide enough for two vehicles in most places. Watch out for several washboard sections and three sand washes (at 16, 18 and 20 miles) where your vehicle can bottom out if you attempt to cross at high speed.

At 25.4 miles look for a four-way dirt intersection and turn left onto a packed sandy road for 0.8 mile to the well and tub. Note: If you miss the intersection you will soon reach a place where the road runs across a river wash on a cement slab. That slab is two miles beyond the intersection. Turn around and go back.

Roper Lake State Park: This refreshing little gem is within easy walking distance of a lake, campground and rest rooms.

504 ROPER LAKE STATE PARK

■

Route 2, Box 712   (602) 428-6760
Safford, AZ 85546   PR+CRV

A small neatly-constructed outdoor soaking pool in a popular state park surrounded by rolling desert hills. Elevation 3,100 ft. Open all year, 6 A.M. to 10 P.M.

Geothermal mineral water flows from an artesian well at 99º directly into a stone-and-cement pool large enough for six to eight good friends. The water flows through continuously so no chemical treatment is needed. There is a 15 minute limit when other people are waiting. Bathing suits are required.

Facilities at the state park include camping and RV spaces, rest rooms, changing rooms, day-use picnic ramadas, a swimming beach, two stocked lakes for fishing, a boat ramp and nature trails. It is 6.5 miles to all other services in Safford.

Directions: From Safford, drive south on US 666 for six miles, turn left (east) at the sign for Roper Lake State Park and continue 0.5 mile to the park entrance.

Shangri La Resort: The hydrojet pool has a roof for protection from the Arizona sun, especially during the summer months.

505 BUCKHORN MINERAL WELLS

■

5900 East Main St.   (602) 832-1111
Mesa, AZ 85205   PR+MH

An historic, older motel-spa which still offers many traditional hot-mineral-water treatment services. Elevation 1,200 ft. Open all year.

Natural mineral water is pumped from two wells at 130º and 140º, then run through a cooling tower. Facilities include separate men's and women's departments, each containing 12 small, individual rooms with cement tubs. A whirlpool pump is mounted on the side of each tub. The temperature of the tub water may be varied by controlling the proportions of hot and cold water admitted. Tubs are drained, cleaned and refilled after each use so that no chemical treatment is required.

Massage, sweat-wrap therapy and motel rooms are available on the premises. Stores and restaurants are located across the street. Service stations and RV spaces are available within one-half mile.

No credit cards are accepted. Phone for rates, reservations and directions.

506 SHANGRI LA RESORT

□

Box 4343 New River Rte. (602) 465-9416
Phoenix, AZ 85027   PR+MH+CRV

Primarily a membership naturist resort located in a scenic high desert valley 30 miles north of Phoenix. Elevation 2,000 ft. Open all year.

Gas-heated well water, chlorine treated, is used in all pools. A large, shaded, fiberglass hot pool is maintained at 104º. The adjoining swimming pool averages 75-80º. Bathing suits are prohibited in both pools.

Facilities include a large club house, volleyball court, tennis courts and sauna. Lodge rooms, camping spaces, cottages and RV hookups are also available.

Visa and MasterCard are accepted. It is five miles to a restaurant and seven miles to a store and service station.

Note: Being a membership club, Shangri La is not open to the public on a drop-in basis. However, a limited number of guest passes may be issued to qualified visitors. Write or telephone well in advance to make arrangements to visit and to obtain directions.

507   SHEEP BRIDGE HOT SPRING

● **Southeast of Prescott**

Three large, cattle-watering tubs on a ledge above the Verde River, with a view of a three-million-dollar sheep bridge. Elevation 1,400 ft. Open all year.

Natural mineral water flows out of a spring at 99º and is piped to three large metal tubs in which the water gradually cools as it flows through them in series. The apparent local custom is clothing optional.

There are no services available on the premises. A level camping area is 75 yards upstream. It is 50 miles to all other services in Black Canyon City.

Directions: It is possible to reach this spring via a very difficult 4WD route from Carefree. However, the following is the recommended route: From I-17 north of Black Canyon City, take the Bloody Basin off-ramp and drive southeast on FS 269 for 37 miles. This road crosses several stream beds which are usually dry. The first 16 miles to Summit (elevation 4,500 ft.) is a good gravel road. The remaining 21 miles is a poor dirt road, but it is passable by a high-clearance 2WD vehicle. From a parking area at the bridge, walk 75 yards upstream to the soaking tubs.

To locate the campground, drive .3 mile back up from the bridge and look on the north side of the road for the remains of a building foundation. A steep path (4WD only!) leads 150 yards down to a level camping area by the river. The soaking tubs are 75 yards downstream from this area.

Source maps: *Mazatzal Wilderness, Tonto National Forest*; USGS quads, *Brooklyn Park, Bloody Basin, Chalk Mountain.*

▲ *Verde Hot Springs:* The crowds are smaller at this location since the nearest parking has been moved more than a mile away.

---

508   VERDE HOT SPRINGS   (see map)

● **Near the town of Camp Verde**

The surprisingly clean remains of an historic resort which burned down years ago. Located on the west bank of the Verde River in a beautiful, high desert canyon. Elevation 2,800 ft. Open all year, subject to river level and bad-weather road hazards.

Natural mineral water flows out of several riverbank springs at 104º and into small, indoor cement soaking pools. A larger, outdoor cement pool is built over another spring and averages 98º. Twenty feet below, at low water level, are several more springs which feed volunteer-built, rock-and-sand pools. Fifty feet upstream from the large cement pool is a 104º pool in a riverbank cave. The apparent local custom is clothing optional. Conscientious visitors have done a superb job of packing out all trash. Please respect this tradition.

There are no services available on the premises, and it is more than 20 miles to the nearest store, service station, and market. Parking and camping are permitted only in a Forest Service campground one mile south of the Childs Power Plant. Therefore, it is a 1 1/2 mile hike to the river ford at Verde Hot Springs. Check with the ranger station in Camp Verde regarding road conditions and river level before attempting to reach this site.

Source maps: *Coconino National Forest.* USGS *Verde Hot Springs.*

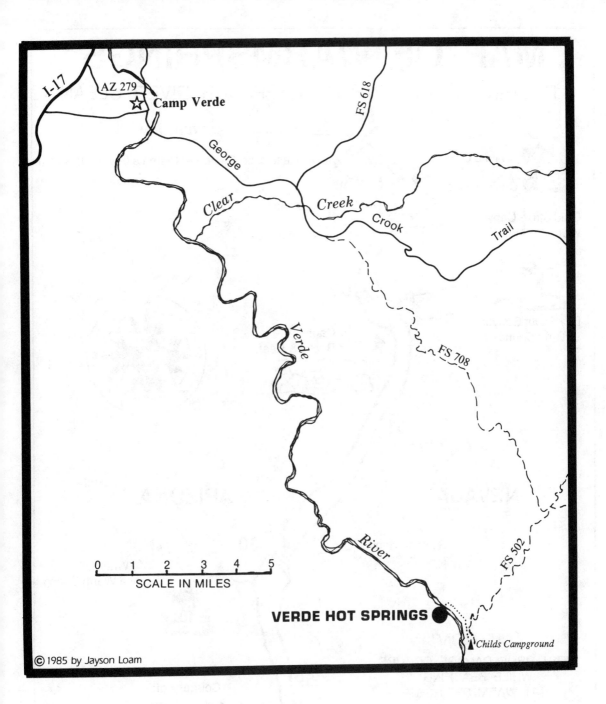

I-17

AZ 279

☆ **Camp Verde**

George

Clear

Creek

Crook

Trail

FS 618

FS 708

Verde

River

FS 502

0   1   2   3   4   5
SCALE IN MILES

VERDE HOT SPRINGS ●

▲*Childs Campground*

ⓒ1985 by Jayson Loam

MAP OF WARMSPRINGS
LITTERING IS UNLAWFUL • KEEP OUR RIVER CLEAN

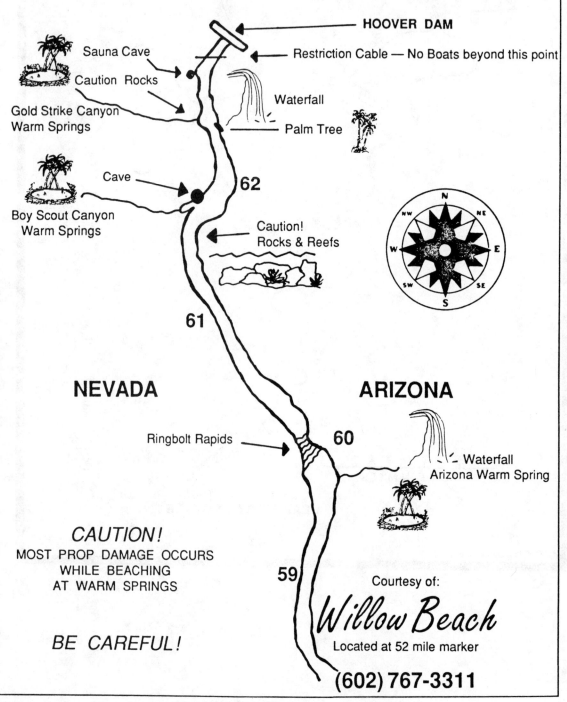

HOOVER DAM

Restriction Cable — No Boats beyond this point

Sauna Cave

Caution Rocks

Gold Strike Canyon
Warm Springs

Waterfall

Palm Tree

Cave

62

Boy Scout Canyon
Warm Springs

Caution!
Rocks & Reefs

61

NEVADA

ARIZONA

Ringbolt Rapids

60

Waterfall
Arizona Warm Spring

CAUTION!
MOST PROP DAMAGE OCCURS
WHILE BEACHING
AT WARM SPRINGS

59

Courtesy of:

Willow Beach

Located at 52 mile marker

BE CAREFUL!

(602) 767-3311

HOT SPRINGS OF THE LOWER COLORADO

Over many centuries flash floods have carved hundreds of spectacular canyons leading into the Colorado River. In three of these canyons, down stream from Hoover Dam, natural mineral water flows out of rocky sidewalls at temperatures up to 125, then gradually cools as it tumbles over a series of waterfalls between sandy-bottom pools. The water is sparkling clear, with no odor and a pleasant taste. In all three of these canyons, volunteers continue to build rock and sand soaking pools, even though most of them are washed away every year by the rainy season flash floods. Elevation 800 ft. Open all year.

Gold Strike Hot Spring: This seep is only one of the several mineral water flows which feed hot waterfalls in the canyon.

Land routes to these springs range from the difficult to the impossible. Most visitors rent an outboard-powered boat at the Willow Beach Resort, which is located eight miles downriver from the springs. Willow Beach also has a ramp for launching your own boat, as well as a restaurant, store, motel and RV spaces. The access road to Willow Beach connects with US 93, 13 miles south of Hoover Dam on the Arizona side of the river.

Rafters and kayakers can obtain a special permit from the Lake Mead National Recreation Area to put-in just below Hoover Dam, float to the various hot springs, and take out at Willow Beach.

Note: The amount of water being released from Hoover Dam is controlled by the Bureau of Reclamation, and may change from hour to hour, which substantially affects the water level in the river. Therefore, it is important that you secure your boat or raft in a manner which will withstand such changes.

509A   GOLD STRIKE HOT SPRINGS
(see map)

● **Near Hoover Dam**

The beach at the bottom of this canyon is within sight of the warning cable stretched across the river just below the dam. One hundred yards up-canyon from the beach, natural mineral water flows out of cliff seeps at 109º into a series of volunteer-built soaking pools.

As you head farther up the canyon you will often be walking in the stream bed bed as well as climbing over sharp rocks, so be prepared with appropriate footwear. Barefoot is definitely not recommended.

The canyon includes several beautiful waterfalls, which can be bypassed only with some strenuous scrambling along smooth rock walls. Near the bottom of the first large falls is a sandy-bottom pool with a water temperature of 100º.

The landmark for this canyon from the river is a pit toilet on the sandy area at the wide canyon mouth. In the river near the canyon mouth there are some large underwater rocks causing rapids. There are also large rocks in the shallow water close to shore, making it difficult to navigate into this canyon entrance. Space for overnight camping at the beach is very limited.

Hiking to this spring is not recommended because it is extremely difficult and dangerous.

509B   BOY SCOUT HOT SPRINGS
(see map)

● **Near Hoover Dam**
A large cave, shaped like a human ear, can be seen on the west riverbank just upstream (north) from this canyon, whose entrance is protected by a land spit which blocks visibility from the south. Landing on the gently sloping sandy beach is easy, but a sudden drop in river level could leave your boat many yards from the water.

The wide sand-and-gravel canyon mouth, has a trickle of 70º water, and plenty of camping space for a group. As you head upstream the canyon narrows and you will often be walking in the stream bed as well as climbing over sharp rocks, so be prepared with appropriate footwear. Barefoot is definitely not recommended. There are several pools and waterfalls in the narrow upper canyon with temperatures up to 104º. The apparent local custom is clothing optional.

There is no safe overland hiking trail to this hot spring.

Boy Scout Hot Springs: Reaching the soaking pools in the upper part of this canyon requires rock scrambling agility.

Ringbolt(Arizona) Hot Springs: Lake Mead National Recreation Area rangers have installed this ladder where the geothermal runoff water forms a high hot waterfall.

509C   RINGBOLT (ARIZONA) HOT SPRINGS
(see map)

● **Near Hoover Dam**

This is the most popular of the three hot springs because it is closest to Willow Beach and downstream from the turbulent water of Ringbolt Rapids. It is 1/8 mile down river from mile marker 60, and two small warning buoys can be seen on a large submerged rock near the beach at the bottom of this canyon. There is no visible stream at the beach because the hot water disappears into the sand a hundred yards before reaching the river.

The long narrow canyon has beautiful rock formations and a few sections which require some scrambling ability. As you head upstream you will often be walking in the stream bed as well as climbing over sharp rocks, so be prepared with appropriate footwear. Barefoot is definitely not recommended. There is a ranger-installed metal ladder at the one major waterfall.

Source springs in the upper canyon flow at 106º, and volunteers have built a series of sandbag or rock-and-sand soaking pools, each with a slightly lower temperature than the one above. The geothermal water is cooled down to approximately 95º by the time it flows over the 25-foot waterfall.

There is a large amount of camping space in the lower canyon and on a dry sandy plateau just south of the canyon mouth.

This is the only spring along the river which has a practical overland route. Hiking directions: From Hoover Dam drive southeast on US 93 to mile post 4.2. and a dirt parking area on your right, at the head of White Rock Canyon. Follow this canyon downhill, through the wash, to the river. Then follow the edge of the river 1/4 mile south to the lower end of Ringbolt Hot Springs canyon and hike upstream to the springs. Distance 2.9 miles, with 800 feet elevation change. The trail is rated moderately strenuous, so allow at least 2.5 hours one way.

▲ This volunteer-built soaking pool in the *Ringbolt Hot Springs* canyon was the site of a small informal birthday party.

Northern California

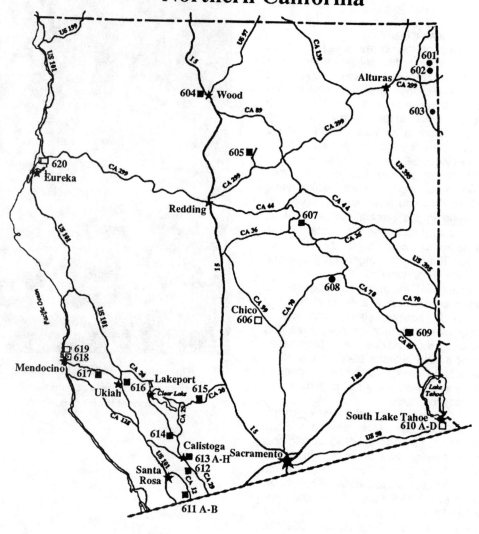

MAP AND DIRECTORY SYMBOLS

● Non-commercial mineral water pool

■ Commercial (fee) mineral water pool

□ Gas-heated tap or well water pool

〜〜〜 Paved highway

- - - Unpaved road

⋯⋯ Hiking route

PR = Tubs or pools for rent by hour, day or treatment

MH = Rooms, cabins or dormitory spaces for rent by day, week or month

CRV = Camping or vehicle parking spaces, some with hookups, for rent by day, week, month or year

601 LEONARD'S HOT SPRING (see map)

● **Near the town of Cedarville**

Abandoned and deteriorated old resort on a barren slope along the east side of Middle Alkali Lake. Elevation 4,500 ft. Open all year.

Natural mineral water flows out of the ground from several springs at a temperature of 150º and cools as it runs toward the lake. A diversion ditch used to carry this water to the resort, but it now flows through a winding ditch fifty yards southeast of the old swimming pool. Volunteers have built shallow soaking pools in the ditch where the water has cooled to approximately 100º. The apparent local custom is clothing optional.

No services are available on the premises. There is an abundance of unmarked level space on which overnight parking is not prohibited. It is nine miles to a service station and all other services.

Source map: USGS *Cedarville*.

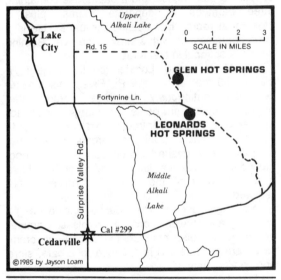

602 GLEN HOT SPRING (see map)

● **Near the town of Cedarville**

Undeveloped cluster of hot springs on a barren slope along the east side of Upper Alkali Lake. Elevation 4,600 ft. Open all year.

Natural mineral water flows out of several springs at 150º and cools as it runs toward the lake. Volunteers have built shallow soaking pools where the water has cooled to approximately 100º. The apparent local custom is clothing optional.

No services are available on the premises. There is a limited amount of unmarked open space on which overnight parking is not prohibited. It is ten miles to a service station and all other services.

Source map: USGS *Cedarville*.

▲ *Eagleville*: Although the rock-and-sand pool is rather shallow, there is a five-foot redwood tub for a deeper soak.

603 EAGLEVILLE HOT SPRING

● **South of the town of Cedarville**

Shallow, primitive soaking pool and tub with a commanding view of Surprise Valley and surrounding mountains. Elevation 4,600 Ft. Open all year.

Natural mineral water flows out of two PVC pipes in the road embankment at 104º. One pipe goes to a volunteer-built rock-and-sand soaking pool and the other pipe goes to an adjacent five-foot redwood tub. The pools are not visible from the road, so the apparent local custom is clothing optional. Local custom also expects new arrivals to await the departure of those already there.

There are no services available on the premises. It is seven miles to Eagleville and 23 miles to Cedarville.

Directions: From Cedarville, on Modoc County Road #1, drive south 15 miles to Eagleville. From the post office, drive seven miles to a slight turnout on the east side of the road and continue 75 yards down the embankment to a dead end. Walk 135 yards north to pool and tub.

▼ *Glen Hot Spring:* Volunteers have dammed and widened this ditch to form a pool.

604　STEWART MINERAL SPRINGS
4617 Stewart Springs Rd.

■ 　　　　　　　　　　　(800) 322-9223
　　　Weed, CA 96094　　　PR+MH+CRV

A well-kept rustic retreat available .to individuals or groups for special events or seminars. Located on a mountain stream in a green canyon northwest of Mt. Shasta. Elevation 3,900 ft. Open March through November on a reservation basis only.

Natural mineral water is pumped from a well at 40º and propane heated as needed. There are 12 individual bathtubs and larger tubs in private rooms. Water temperature in each tub is controlled, as desired, by mixing cold and hot mineral water. Tubs are drained and refilled after each use, so no chemical treatment of the water is necessary. The outdoor hydropool is filled with creek water, filtered, chlorinated and heated to 102º. Bathing suits are required in public areas.

Facilities include rooms, restaurant, bar (beer and wine), camping spaces and partial-hookup RV spaces. Massage is available by appointment. Major credit cards are accepted. It is seven miles to a store, service station and public bus. Special pickup at the bus depot and at the Weed airport is available by arrangement.

Directions: From I-5 north of Weed, take the Edgewood exit and follow signs four miles north on Stewart Springs Road to the resort.

▼ *Big Bend Hot Springs*: Runoff from the lower hot spring gradually cools as it flows toward the Pit River through a series of rock pools.

605　BIG BEND HOT SPRINGS
　　196 Hot Springs Row　　(916) 337-6680
■　Big Bend, CA 96011　　　PR+MH+CRV

The remains of an historical resort being improved and operated by a cooperative self-sufficient Essene Community. Located 50 miles northeast of Redding on the tree-shaded south bank of the Pit River. Elevation 2,000 ft. Open all year.

Natural mineral water flows from three springs at 180º.

(1) Indian Springs. Located ten feet above the level of the nearby Pit River, the flow from this spring cools as it meanders through a series of shallow pools created by volunteers from riverbed rocks. Bathing suits are optional in this area and in the adjoining river.

(2) Main spring. Located on a plateau 50 feet above the river level, this major, controlled flow supplies a greenhouse and a bathhouse containing three bathtubs in separate rooms, plus a steambath room. Just outside the bathhouse is a large fiberglass tub with a view of the river. Bathing suits are optional in these tubs.

(3) Minor spring. Located on the edge of a plateau 50 feet above the Pit River, this smaller flow runs continuously into three interconnected natural stone/cement pools, each large enough for six persons. Faucet-controlled cold creek water is added to each pool to produce whatever temperature is desired by occupants. Each pool has seating at various depths, and all of them have a superb view of the river. Bathing suits are required.

Massage, cabins, RV spaces and overnight camping are available on the premises. Seminar programs are also open to the public. No credit cards are accepted. It is 1/4 mile to a cafe, store and service station.

Directions: From I-5 in Redding, go 35 miles east on CA 299, then turn north 15 miles to the town of Big Bend, which is at the end of the pavement. Look for Big Bend Hot Springs sign 200 yards south of Big Bend store.

Even the developed pools at *Big Bend* seem to fit perfectly in the natural surroundings.

Drakesbad Guest Ranch: The source hot springs, located on the slope above the ranch, feed the large swimming pool.

606 CHICO HOT TUB HAVEN
Ninth and Salem   (916) 895-0409
Chico, CA 95926   PR

Hot tub rental establishment off the main thoroughfare (Highway 32) in Chico. Open all year.

The nearby creek can be heard in the four private enclosed outdoor tubs equipped with dressing rooms and showers. The tubs are chlorine treated and maintained at temperatures from 100-104º.

Stereos (bring your favorite tapes), radios and beverages are available on the premises. Visa and MasterCard are accepted. Phone for rates, reservations and directions.

607 DRAKESBAD GUEST RANCH
c/o California Guest Services, Inc.
2150 Main St. #5   (916) 529-1512
Red Bluff, CA 96080   MH

A rustic mountain ranch/resort with a mineral-water swimming pool, plus horses and guides for riding and hiking. Located in a superb mountain meadow within the boundaries of Lassen Volcanic National Park. Elevation 5,700 ft. Open first part of June to first part of October.

Natural mineral water flows out of two springs at temperatures of 85º and 125º and is piped to the pool. The swimming pool is maintained in the 80s during the day and over 100º at night by mixing the two hot water flows. Pool flow is shut off after midnight, and chlorine is added to control algae growth; but chlorine content reduces rapidly when flow-through is resumed the following day. Bathing suits are required. The pool is available to registered guests only. No day use is permitted.

Facilities include lodge, rooms, cabins, bungalows and dining room (all kerosene lit). Saddle horses and guides are available by the hour. Visa and MasterCard are accepted. It is 17 miles to RV spaces, store and service station. Telephone for reservations.

Directions: From CA 36 in the town of Chester take Warner Valley Road northwest to resort, which is at the end of the road.

608 WOODY'S FEATHER RIVER HOT SPRINGS

P.O. Box 7
Twain, CA 95984

(916) 283-4115
PR+MH+RV

Primarily a fishing and hunting resort, this site does have two small soaking pools on the north bank of the Feather River, where you can also pan for gold. The resort is located in the tree-covered upper Feather River Canyon. Elevation 2,700 ft. Open all year.

Natural mineral water flows directly into two cement pools at 99º and 102º. No chemical treatment is added. Clothing is optional in the pools and in the adjoining river.

Facilities include motel rooms, RV spaces, restaurant and bar. No credit cards are accepted. It is three miles to a store and 15 miles to a service station.

Directions: On CA 70, go four miles west from the Quincy-Greenville "Y."

One of a variety of pools at *Sierra Hot Springs.* This one, surrounded by tall pines, offers a lovely view across an Alpine valley.

Woody's Feather River Hot Springs: Located 30 yards from a highway and a tavern, this is a convenient informal recreation spot.

609 SIERRA HOT SPRINGS

P.O. Box 366
Sierraville, CA 96126

(916) 994-3773
PR+MH+C

A 500-acre rustic resort which is being restored and expanded by a nonprofit spiritual community. Public use of the facilities is welcome on a space-available basis. Elevation 5,000 ft. Open all year.

Natural mineral water flows out of several springs at temperatures up to 112º. On a wooded slope a variety of tubs at several temperatures use flow-through mineral water without chemical treatment: (a) three cement soaking pools, 110º, 106º, 102º; (b) bathtub, 102º; (c) redwood hot tubs, 102º, and (d) galvanized tubs. Clothing is optional in all pool areas.

Hotel and lodge rooms, dormitory accommodations, camping spaces, and massage are available on the premises. Also available is restaurant, or facilities to cook your own food. Most major credit cards are accepted. It is two miles to a store and service station, .

Directions: From the intersection of CA 89 and CA 49 in Sierraville, follow CA 49 east to Lemon Canyon Rd., which runs along the north edge of the airport; then turn right on Campbell Hot Springs Rd., which runs along the east edge of the airport, and continue into the foothills to the main office.

610A NEPHELE

☐ 1169 Ski Run Blvd.   (916) 544-8130
So. Lake Tahoe, CA 95729   PR

Combination bar, restaurant and rent-a-tub establishment, located between the lake and a ski run.

Four private, enclosed outdoor pools are for rent to the public. Using gas-heated tap water and treated with bromine, the pools are maintained at 102º. Bar service (but not food) is available at poolside.

A bar and restaurant are available on the premises. There are dinner-and-soak combination discounts. Visa, MasterCard and American Express are accepted. Phone for rates, reservations and directions.

Nephele: Bar service to a private outdoor hot pool is available day and night. ►

▲ *Pacifica Lodge*: Crystal chandeliers and an in-room pool may be rented overnight or longer for private use.

610B PACIFICA LODGE

☐ 931 Park Ave.   (916) 544-4131
So. Lake Tahoe, CA 95729   MH/P

Large motel with some special rooms containing fiberglass hydropools. Located a few blocks from the beach and from the Nevada state line.

Gas-heated tap water is used in six in-room pools which may be rented overnight or longer for private use. These pools are drained and refilled after each check-out, so no chemical water treatment is necessary.

The outdoor communal swimming pool is maintained at 80º and uses gas-heated tap water treated with chlorine. All pools are for registered guests only. Visa, MasterCard and American Express are accepted. Phone for rates, reservations and directions.

610C TAHOE HACIENDA MOTEL

☐ 3820 Hwy 50   (916) 541-3805
So. Lake Tahoe, CA 95705   MH+PR

Major motel with a dozen rooms containing hydropools. Located on the south side of Hwy 50.

Gas-heated tap water is used in 12 fiberglass pools in rooms which may be rented for private use overnight or longer. These pools are drained and refilled after each check-out, so no chemical water treatment is needed. Temperature in each pool is adjustable to the guests' preference.

The outdoor communal swimming pool (approximately 80º) is open June through September, and the outdoor communal hydropool (approximately 103º) is open all year. Both outdoor pools require chlorination. Bathing suits are required in outdoor pools. Visa, MasterCard, American Express and Carte Blanche are accepted. Phone for rates, reservations and directions.

610D PINEWOOD LODGE

☐ 3818 Hwy 50   (916) 544-3319
So. Lake Tahoe, CA 95729   MH+PR

Small motel with one separate room containing a hot tub, sauna and shower. Located on the south side of Hwy 50.

Gas-heated tap water treated with chlorine is used in the redwood tub, and water temperature is maintained at 100º. The tub/sauna room may be rented by the hour or negotiated in connection with regular motel room registration.

Visa, MasterCard and American Express are accepted. Phone for rates, reservations and directions.

611A SONOMA MISSION INN & SPA
■ P.O. Box 1447   (707) 938-9000
Sonoma, CA 95476   MH

Luxuriously restored resort providing multiple kinds of beauty and health packages for your benefit and enjoyment in a beautiful, romantic setting.

Mineral water flows out of the source at 135° and is piped to one large outdoor and one large indoor whirlpool tub, lightly treated with bromine and refilled daily. The water in both pools is maintained at 102°. The mineral water is also used to fill the two outdoor swimming pools, treated lightly with bromine and refilled daily. The large pool is maintained at 82° and the spa pool at 92°. Mineral water showers are also available in the spa.

Beautifully appointed rooms, a gourmet restaurant, a cafe, coed exercise and spa facilities, and tennis courts are available on the premises. In addition, over 40 different spa packages are offered. Call for rates, reservations, directions and details.

Upscale all the way with health and luxury as the theme, the *Sonoma Mission Inn* offers complete packages and romantic settings.

White Sulphur Springs Resort: A soak in this chlorine-free pool, and a picnic in a redwood grove by a running stream, can be a welcome relief from crowds of visitors who flock to the Napa Valley wine country.

611B AGUA CALIENTE MINERAL SPRINGS

17350 Vailetti Dr.   **(707) 996-6822**
Sonoma, CA 95476   **PR**

A summertime plunge and picnic grounds in the middle of the Sonoma Valley. Elevation 100 ft. Open summer months only.

Natural mineral water is pumped from a well at 96º and piped to a swimming pool which averages 86º and to a hydropool which averages 95º. The adjoining diving pool and wading pool, averaging 70º, are filled with unheated tap water; both pools are treated with chlorine and are drained and filled every day. Bathing suits are required.

A seasonal snack bar is available on the premises. No credit cards are accepted. It is less than one mile to a store, service station and all other services.

Directions: From the city of Sonoma, go three miles north on CA 12 and watch for Agua Caliente signs.

612 WHITE SULPHUR SPRINGS RESORT

3100 White Sulphur Springs Rd.
    (707) 963-8858
St. Helena, CA 94574   **PR+MH**

Historic, 330-acre, resort surrounded by the beauty of the Napa Valley. Elevation 400 ft. Open all year.

Natural mineral water flows out of several springs at various temperatures up to 95º and is piped to one outdoor soaking pool which operates on flow-through basis requiring no chemical treatment and is maintained at 85-87º. Also available is a 20-person jet tub, filled with chlorine-treated spring water, maintained at an average temperature of 103º. All pools are available to the public for day use, as well as to registered guests. Bathing suits are required.

Extensive hiking trails on the wooded premises extend through forested canyons and fern-lined creeks. Other facilities include new health center which offers massage, and herbal and mud wraps. Overnight accommodations include cottages and inn rooms. Fully equipped meeting rooms and kitchen facilities are available. The redwood grove is a perfect setting for weddings, picnics or family reunions. Visa and MasterCard are accepted. It is three miles to central St. Helena and all other services.

Directions: From CA 29 in the center of St. Helena, drive three miles west on Spring St. to the resort.

Calistoga Spa Hot Springs: The outdoor pool complex and the health/fitness services in the men's and women's bathhouses are available to the public.

All eight of the following locations are in or near the town of Calistoga, which is on CA 29 in Napa County, Elevation 400 ft. All of them are open all year and are one to ten blocks from a store, cafe, service station, public bus and the RV campground operated by Napa County at the Fairgrounds.

All of them have their own hot wells, and offer soaking and swimming pools containing natural mineral water treated with chlorine. Unless otherwise noted, resorts with pool facilities offer them for day use except on busy weekends and holidays. Soaking tubs in bathhouses are drained and filled after each use so that no chemical treatment of the water is necessary. Bathing suits are required in all public places.

613A CALISTOGA SPA HOT SPRINGS

■ 1006 Washington St. (707) 942-6269
Calistoga, CA 94515 PR+MH

Outdoor soaking pool, 100º; outdoor swimming pool, 83º; and outdoor wading pool, 90º. Covered hydropool, 105º. Indoor men's and women's bathhouses, each containing four individual tubs, two mud baths and three steambaths.

Rooms, massage, blanket wraps, steambaths, aerobic classes and workout rooms are available on the premises. Visa, MasterCard and American Express are accepted.

▲ *Dr. Wilkinson's Hot Springs*: One of the available choices is this quiet indoor soaking pool, ringed by tropical plants.

613B DR. WILKINSON'S HOT SPRINGS
1507 Lincoln Ave. **(707) 942-6257**
■ **Calistoga, CA 94515** **PR+MH**

Two outdoor mineral pools, 82º and 92º; one tropical-foliage indoor mineral pool, 104º. Indoor men's and women's bathhouses, each containing four individual tubs, two mud baths and a steambath.

Rooms, massage, mud baths, blanket wraps and skin care salon are available on the premises. Visa and MasterCard and American Express are accepted.

▲ *Golden Haven Hot Springs:* These covered pools can be used in all kinds of weather.

613C GOLDEN HAVEN HOT SPRINGS
1713 Lake St. **(707) 942-6793**
■ **Calistoga, CA 94515** **PR+MH**

Enclosed mineral water swimming pool, 80º; covered hydropool, 102º.

Rooms, massage, facials, mud baths for couples and European body wraps are available on the premises. Visa and MasterCard are accepted.

▲ *Hideaway Cottages:* These pools are for the exclusive use of registered guests.

▲ *Indian Springs:* The plume of steam just beyond the pool comes from the geothermal source, a flowing artesian well.

613D HIDEAWAY COTTAGES
■ 1412 Fairway   (707) 942-4108
Calistoga, CA 94515   MH

Outdoor swimming pool, 82º, and hydropool, 104º. Reserved for registered guests; no day use.

Cottages are available. Visa, American Express and MasterCard are accepted.

613E INDIAN SPRINGS
■ 1712 Lincoln Ave.   (707) 942-4913
Calistoga, CA 94515   PR+MH

Outdoor, Olympic-size swimming pool, 88-102º. Open all year. Indoor men's and women's bathhouses, each containing five one-person mud or mineral water soaking tubs and a steam room.

Rooms and massage are available on the premises. Visa and MasterCard are accepted.

613F CALISTOGA VILLAGE INN AND SPA
■ 1880 Lincoln Ave.   (707) 942-0991
Calistoga, CA 94515   PR+MH

Outdoor swimming pool, 80-85º, and wading pool, 90-95º. Enclosed hydropool, 100-105º. Indoor men's and women's bathhouses, each containing two hydrotherapy tubs, two mud baths, two steam cabinets and a sauna.

Massage, facials, herbal bath, and salt scrub are available on the premises. Facilities include rooms and conference meeting rooms. Visa American Express and MasterCard are accepted.

▼ *Calistoga Village Inn and Spa:* All tubs are drained and cleaned after each use.

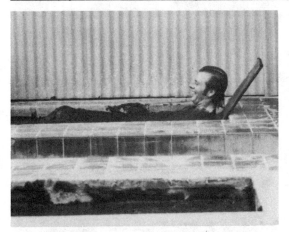

Nance's Hot Springs: Traditional mud baths are available in both the men's and women's bathhouses at this location.

International Spa: Located on the grounds of the Roman Spa, this alert enterprise has designed its equipment and its services for the enjoyment of couples.

613G   NANCE'S HOT SPRINGS

1614 Lincoln Ave.   (707) 942-6211
■ **Calistoga, CA 94515   PR+MH**

Indoor hydropool, 103º. Indoor men's and women's bathhouses, containing four individual tubs (up to 110º), three mud baths and two steambaths in each section.

Quality lodgings feature some non-smoking rooms, rooms for the handicapped, some rooms with kitchens, and two rooms with large whirlpool tubs. Massage is also available on the premises. Glider rentals are available at the adjoining airport. Visa, MasterCard and American Express are accepted.

613H   ROMAN SPA

1300 Washington St.   (707) 942-4441
■ **Calistoga, CA 94515   PR+MH**

Outdoor swimming pool, 92-95º, and hydropool, 104º. Indoor hydropool, 100º. Motel rooms available.

International Spa, under separate management, offers massage, reflexology, acupressure, coed mud and enzyme baths, mineral baths, hydrotherapy massage, herbal blanket wrap, herbal facials and aroma therapy baths and massage. Visa, MasterCard and American Express are accepted.

Roman Spa: In the room just beyond the outdoor hydropool is an indoor hydropool.

Harbin Hot Springs: The sundeck and one of the overnight accommodation buildings are visible on the far side of the pool.

At *Harbin Hot Springs* it is possible for a mother to simultaneously enjoy soaking in a hot pool and breast feeding her baby.

The several kinds of hot pools available at *Harbin Hot Springs* is supplemented by this invigorating cold water pool.

614 HARBIN HOT SPRINGS (see map)
P.O. Box 782   (707) 987-2477
Middletown, CA 95461   PR+MH+CRV

Large historical resort being restored and expanded by a new age nonprofit organization with a major residential program. Located in a rugged foothill canyon south of Clear Lake. Elevation 1,500 ft. Open all year.

Natural mineral water with mild mineral content flows out of the ground at 120º and is piped to several soaking pools and a swimming pool. An enclosed cement pool has an average temperature of 110-115º, an adjoining cement pool has an average temperature of 100-104º, and the swimming pool ranges from 60-70º. All pools operate on a frequent cleaning and flow-through basis, so no chemical treatment is needed. Clothing is optional everywhere within the grounds except in the kitchen and dining room.

Facilities include day use of pools, rooms, camping and RV spaces, four conference buildings, and a restaurant where vegetarian meals are optional. Massage and massage training in a state-accredited school are available on the premises. Visa and MasterCard are accepted. It is four miles to a store and service station.

Phone for rates, reservations and directions.

▼ *Clothing is optional everywhere on the grounds of Harbin Hot Springs except in the kitchen, dining room and deck.*

▲ *Wilbur Hot Springs*: The structure above the swimming pool is filled with large soaking pools at various temperatures.

615 WILBUR HOT SPRINGS
3375 Wilbur Springs Rd.

(916) 473-2306
Williams, CA 95987   PR+MH

A self-styled "Health Sanctuary" 22 miles from the nearest town, with an abundance of hot mineral water. The large, multi-temperature soaking pools, the sundecks, and the restored turn-of-the-century hotel are located in the foothills of the western Sacramento Valley. Elevation 1,350 ft. Open all year.

Natural mineral water flows out of several springs at 140º, through a series of large concrete soaking pools under an A-frame structure, and into an outdoor swimming pool. Soaking pool temperatures are approximately 115º, 105º and 95º, with the swimming pool kept warm in the winter and cool in the summer. The water is not chemically treated. Bathing suits are optional in pool areas only, required elsewhere.

Massage, rooms, dormitory and communal kitchen are available on the premises. Visa and MasterCard are accepted. It is 22 miles to a restaurant, store and service station.

Note: Please no drop-in visitors. Phone first for reservations and confirmation of any services or uses.

Directions: From Interstate 5 in Williams, go west on CA 20 to the intersection with CA 16. A few yards west of that intersection, take gravel road heading north and west for approximately five miles, and follow signs.

Vichy Springs Resort and Inn: Historic facilities include outdoor and indoor concrete two-person soaking tubs.

This large modern soaking pool is a recent addition to the choices at *Vichy Springs*.

616   VICHY SPRINGS RESORT AND INN
2605 Vichy Springs Rd.
(707) 462-9515; FAX (707) 462-9516
Ukiah, CA 95842   PR+MH+RV

Historic 682-acre resort in the Ukiah Valley foothills area of Mendocino County, famous for its warm and naturally carbonated mineral water, which is bottled and sold to the public. Elevation 900 ft. Open all year.

Naturally carbonated mineral water flows out of the springs at 90º and through traditional redwood pipes to ten enclosed, two-person concrete soaking tubs. These tubs are drained and filled after each use, so no chemical treatment is necessary. There is one large, communal soaking tub in which the water is treated with ozone and heated to 104º. The Olympic-size swimming pool contains ozone-treated water maintained at approximately 80º during the summer. All tubs and pools are available to the public for day use as well as to registered guests at any time.

Facilities include a tree-shaded four-acre central lawn ringed by country-style cottages and rooms, overnight parking for self-contained RVs, a tree-ringed pond, a running stream and a 30-minute hike to a user-friendly waterfall. Massage and facials and bed and breakfast are available by appointment on the premises. Visa, MasterCard and American Express are accepted. It is five miles to a campground and three miles to the center of Ukiah.

Phone for brochure, rates, reservations and directions.

617 ORR HOT SPRINGS

13201 Orr Springs Rd.   (707) 462-6277
Ukiah, CA 95482   PR+MH+C

A charming, older resort being continually improved offering friendly informality and colorful flowerbeds. It is located on a wooded creek, 35 miles inland from the ocean. Elevation 800 ft. Open all year.

Natural mineral water flows out of several springs at 100º and is piped to a swimming pool, an indoor soaking pool, and four bathtubs in private rooms. The swimming pool averages 70º. The indoor tub and outdoor soaking pool are housed in a bathhouse built in 1858. Some of the water is heated to 105º and pumped to an enclosed redwood tub which overflows into an adjoining shallow outdoor soaking pool famed for its stargazing. All pools operate on a flow-through basis, so no chemical treatment is added. Clothing is optional everywhere on the grounds.

Facilities include a sauna, communal kitchen, rooms, dormitory and tent spaces along the creek. Massage is available by reservation. Space is limited, so telephone first for any use of the facilities. Visa and MasterCard are accepted. It is 13 miles of steep and winding roads to a restaurant, store and service station.

Directions: From Route 101 in Ukiah, take the North State Street exit, drive 1/4 mile north to Orr Springs Road, turn west and drive 13 miles to the resort.

Orr Hot Springs: Grass and greenery around this warm swimming pool give it the feel and appearance of a quiet country oasis.

At *Orr Hot Springs* the outdoor massage area adjoins the outdoor soaking pool.

▲ *Sweetwater Gardens:* This is one of the authentic Northern California communal hot tubs which helped make the idea popular.

There is also this smaller private-space hot tub available at *Sweetwater Gardens.*

618 SWEETWATER GARDENS
□ 955 Ukiah St.   (707) 937-4140
Mendocino, CA 95460   PR+MH

Rustic rent-a-tub establishment featuring natural wood tubs, walls and decking with hanging greenery. Located on the coast of Northern California.

Pools are for rent to the public and use gas-heated tap water treated with bromine. One private enclosure can be rented by the hour. The water temperature is maintained at 104º, and a sauna is included. One private suite can be rented by the hour and also by the night. The water temperature is maintained at 104º, and a sauna is included. One communal hydropool is available at a day-rate charge. The water temperature is maintained at 104º, and a sauna is included.

Special features: Sweetwater has a variety of unique lodging options including ocean view units, cottages and romantic water tower rooms. Bathing suits are optional everywhere. Professional massage offering a wide range of bodywork is available on the premises. Visa and MasterCard are accepted. Phone for rates, reservations and directions.

▲ *The Garden Cottage*: A private tub and a private cottage in the Mendocino area makes for a romantic weekend.

▲ *Finnish County Sauna and Hot Tubs*: Hot tubs made of Jarrah wood resulted from the search for a tub material which was more resistant to hot water than redwood.

519 (CASPAR) THE GARDEN COTTAGE

45310 Pacifica Dr.   (707) 964-6456
Caspar, CA 95420   MH

Beautifully furnished cottage with private outdoor hot tub midway between Mendocino and Fort Bragg. Open all year.

Private hot tub using gas-heated well water treated with chlorine, is maintained at 104º, and along with a sauna are included in the rental of a cottage for two or the cottage with bedroom for four. Clothing is optional in private spaces.

Facilities include a completely equipped kitchen, VCR, stereo, telephone and wood heat. No credit cards are accepted. Phone for rates, reservations and directions.

520 FINNISH COUNTRY SAUNA & TUBS

5th and J St.   (707) 822-2228
Arcata, CA 95521   PR

A charming pond surrounded by grass-roofed Finnish saunas, outdoor hot tubs and a European-style coffeehouse in a small northern California coastal town. Elevation 50 ft. Open all year.

Tubs are for rent to the public and use gas-heated tap water treated with bromine. There are six private, outdoor Jarrah-wood hot tubs rented by the half-hour and maintained at 104º. Bathing suits are optional in private spaces.

Facilities include cabins, two rentable private saunas, and Cafe Mokha, a coffee house serving espresso and juices. No credit cards are accepted. Phone for rates, reservations and directions.

Central California

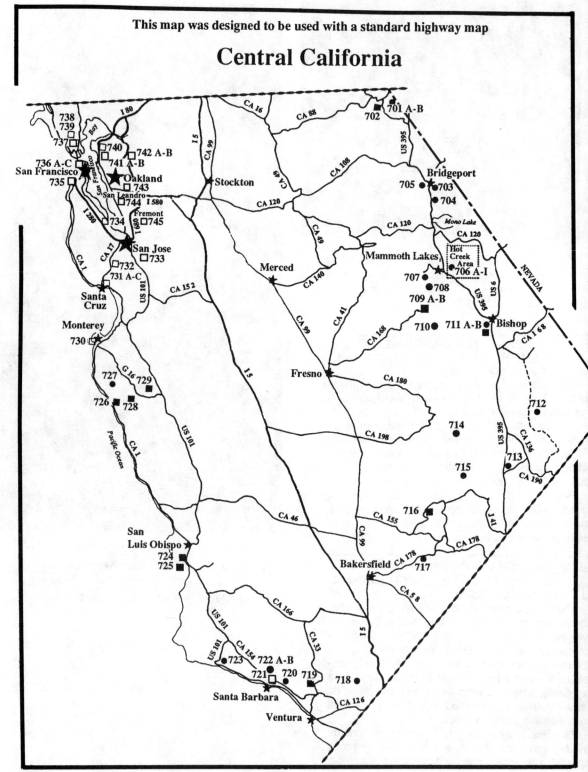

701A   RIVERSIDE HOT SPRINGS

●

Near the town of Markleeville

One of two primitive hot springs on a remote section of the East Carson River in Toiyabe National Forest. The only access is by raft or kayak. Elevation 5,000 ft. Open during rafting season, which is approximately May, June and July.

Natural mineral water emerges from several springs at 107º and cools as it flows toward the river. The temperature of the water drops to approximately 104º by the time it reaches some shallow pools near an eight-foot cliff at the edge of the river. The apparent local custom is clothing optional.

There are no services available on the premises. One- and two-day raft trips (Class II rapids) conducted by experienced guides are available locally. For information and/or pre-trip meals and lodging, contact Sorenson's Resort, (916) 694-2203.

These springs are not shown on any Forest Service or USGS map but are well known to raft trip guides.

Riverside Hot Springs: The raft trip leader is demonstrating how to enter a geothermal waterfall while fully dressed.

701B HOT SHOWERBATH

● **Near the town of Markleeville**

The other primitive hot spring on the East Carson River, approximately one mile downstream from Riverside Hot Springs.

Natural mineral water flows out of a spring at 110º and cools to approximately 98º before dropping over a 20-foot bank into a canyon which extends 500 yards west of the river. The apparent local custom is clothing-optional.

See the preceding listing, RIVERSIDE HOT SPRINGS, for information on access and services.

▲ *Hot Showerbath:* A 500 yard hike from the East Carson River is needed to reach this head-pounding stream of hot mineral water.

702 GROVER HOT SPRINGS

Box 188   (916) 694-2248
■ Markleeville, CA 96120   PR (free) +CRV

Conventional swimming pool and soaking pool next to a major state campground and picnic area, located in a wooded mountain valley. Elevation 6,000 ft. Open all year.

Natural mineral water flows out of several springs at 147º and into a holding pond from which it is piped to the pool area. The soaking pool, using natural mineral water treated with bromine, is maintained at approximately 103º. The swimming pool, using creek water treated with chlorine, is maintained at 70-80º. A heat exchanger is used to simultaneously cool down the mineral water and warm up the creek water. Admission is on a first-come, first-served basis, and the official capacity limit of 50 persons in the hot pool plus 25 in the cold pool is reached early every day during the summer. Bathing suits are required.

Campground spaces are available by prior reservation, as with all other California state parks. Cross-country skiers are encouraged to camp in the picnic area during the winter and to ski in to use the soaking pool. It is four miles to the nearest restaurant, motel and service station.

Location: On Alpine County Road E4, 4 1/2 miles west of Markleeville. Follow the signs.

▲ *Grover Hot Springs:* If the pool area is full when you reach the gate, all you can do is stand in line until someone leaves.

Grover Hot Springs State Park includes all of this beautiful alpine valley in addition to the pools fed by hot springs.

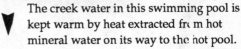

The creek water in this swimming pool is kept warm by heat extracted from hot mineral water on its way to the hot pool.

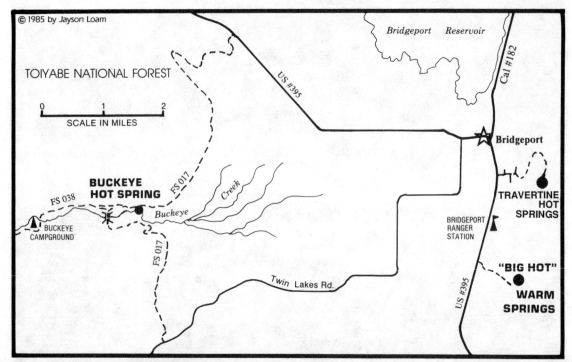

TOIYABE NATIONAL FOREST

Bridgeport Reservoir

US #395

Cal #182

0   1   2
SCALE IN MILES

BUCKEYE HOT SPRING

FS 017

Creek

FS 038

Buckeye

BUCKEYE CAMPGROUND

FS 017

Twin Lakes Rd.

US #395

Bridgeport

BRIDGEPORT RANGER STATION

TRAVERTINE HOT SPRINGS

"BIG HOT"

WARM SPRINGS

Travertine Hot Springs: This shallow pool has a view of a large travertine deposit.

703   TRAVERTINE HOT SPRINGS
   (see map)

● **Southeast of the town of Bridgeport**

An unusual group of volunteer-built soaking pools on large travertine ridges with commanding views of the High Sierra. Located two miles from the center of Bridgeport. Elevation 6,700 ft. Open all year.

The flow of natural mineral water (130-160º) out of several geothermal fissures can be interrupted, or shifted to a new outlet, by underground movement resulting from local earthquakes. The scalding water is channeled to a series of volunteer-built soaking pools in which the individual pool temperatures are controlled by temporarily diverting the hot water inflow as needed. The apparent local custom is clothing optional.

There are no services, but there is level ground on which overnight parking is not prohibited. All other services are available within two miles in Bridgeport.

Directions: From Bridgeport, drive 0.6 mile south on US 395 and turn east on paved Jack Sawyer Rd. Within the next 0.3 mile there are three unmarked forks. At the first fork (on the left), keep going straight. At the second fork where the paved road goes off to the right, keep going straight on the dirt road. At the third fork (on the left), bear right on the road which winds up into the hills. Drive 0.4 mile to fourth fork (on the left, signed *Bridgeport Borrow Pit*). Continue straight ahead for 0.7 mile to a parking area near a large soaking pool. To reach the other pools, walk downhill 100 yards southwest.

▲ Volunteers excavated this *Travertine Hot Springs* Big Pool out of mineral deposits built up over thousands of years.

▲ In the *Travertine Hot Springs* area, small earthquakes continually create and terminate geothermal springs. This is the latest volunteer-built pool, excavated at the site of a newly-flowing hot spring.

▲ *"Big Hot" Warm Springs:* You can soak safely along the shallow edge of the big pool but the center depth exceeds 20 feet.

704 "BIG HOT" WARM SPRINGS
(see map on preceding page)
● **Near the town of Bridgeport**

A cluster of unimproved warm spring pools with a great view of the High Sierra. Elevation 7,000 ft. Open all year, but the unmaintained dirt road is not passable in winter.

Natural mineral water flows up from many seeps and holes at various temperatures up to 93º. Air temperatures and wind conditions affect the average water temperature. The largest pool is big enough for two dozen persons and is more than ten-feet deep in the center. The apparent local custom is clothing optional.

There are no services available on the premises. There is a substantial amount of unmarked open space on which overnight parking is not prohibited. The final 200 yards of road goes up a steep bank suitable only for walking or 4WD vehicles. Please be sure to close any gates you open. It is four miles to the nearest store, restaurant, motel and service station.

Source map: USGS *Bodie.*

705 BUCKEYE HOT SPRING
(see map on preceding page)
● **Near the town of Bridgeport**

Delightful hot spring in a superb natural setting on the north bank of Buckeye Creek in Toiyabe National Forest. One of the best. Elevation 6,900 ft. Open all year; not accessible by road in winter.

Natural mineral water flows out of the ground at 135º, runs over a large cliff built up by mineral deposits, and drops into the creek. Volunteers have built loosely constructed rock pools along the edge of the creek below the hot waterfall. The pool temperature is controlled by admitting more or less cold water from the creek. The apparent local custom is clothing optional.

There are no services on the premises. There is a parking turnout on the south side of the road on the bluff above the springs. The easiest route to the soaking pools is to follow the unofficial path down the slope from the turnout.

There is another small outflow of hot geothermal water on the bluff near the parking area. Volunteers have dug a shallow soaking pool which maintains a temperature of approximately 100º. It is near the foot of a tree located in the upstream direction from the parking area.

Three hundred yards upstream from the parking area are several acres of unmarked open space along the road on which overnight parking is not prohibited. It is one mile to a Forest Service campground and nine miles to a restaurant, motel, store and service station in Bridgeport.

Source maps: *Toiyabe National Forests;* USGS *Matterhorn Peak.*

Buckeye Hot Spring water cascades into the first of several volunteer-built rock pools along the edge of the creek. The fisherman is trying for a few trout before joining his family in the soaking pools.

Buckeye Hot Spring: This small volunteer-built pool is on the slope overlooking Buckeye Creek. The main geothermal flow has built up a white mineral deposit on the creek bank in the center of the photo.

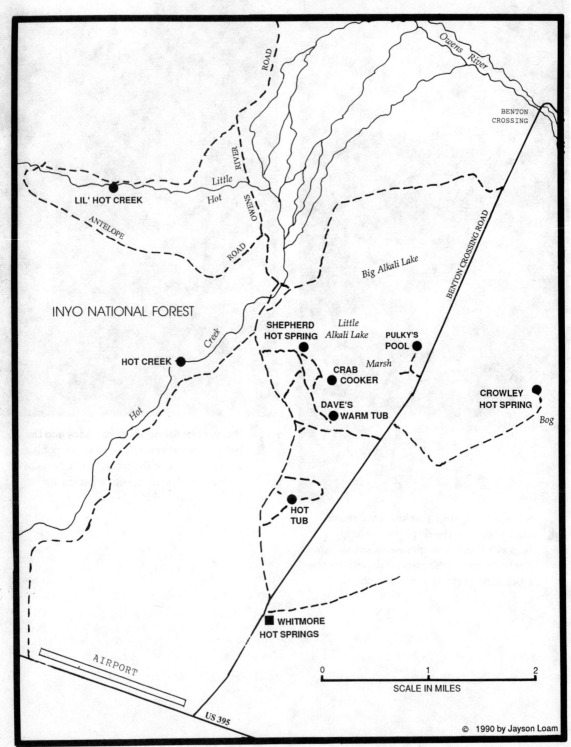

THE HOT CREEK AREA
MOTHER LODE OF THE EASTERN SIERRA

ROAD

Owens River

BENTON
CROSSING

RIVER

Little

Hot

OWENS

LIL' HOT CREEK

ANTELOPE

ROAD

Big Alkali Lake

BENTON CROSSING ROAD

INYO NATIONAL FOREST

Creek

SHEPHERD
HOT SPRING

Little
Alkali Lake

PULKY'S
POOL

HOT CREEK

Marsh

CRAB
COOKER

CROWLEY
HOT SPRING

Hot

DAVE'S
WARM TUB

Bog

HOT
TUB

WHITMORE
HOT SPRINGS

AIRPORT

0   1   2

SCALE IN MILES

US 395

© 1990 by Jayson Loam

Motorists on US 395 in Mono County see a geothermal power plant beside the highway just east· of the famous skiing town of Mammoth Lakes. A few miles father east there are numerous fumeroles and hot springs, some of which erupt up through the bottom of the well-named Hot Creek.

In general, the area is open all year, but, at an altitude of 7,000 feet, heavy snows limit winter access to cross-country skiers and hikers. The official Forest Service Observation Site (Hot Creek) is open only during daylight hours and Whitmore Hot Springs is open only during the summer.

The nearby BLM land is sprinkled with small hot springs which flow into bogs, marshes and alkali lakes. Over the years volunteers have used modern materials to build an impressive group of soaking pools with ingenious methods for controlling water temperature. Overnight parking is not prohibited in the undeveloped portions of the area.

It is ten miles to all other services in the town of Mammoth Lakes.

Source maps: *Inyo National Forest.* USGA *Mt. Morrison.*

Hot Creek: Visitors are warned of the dangers, and then are permitted, during daylight hours, to explore that portion of the creek where hot water mixes with cold.

706A   HOT CREEK   (see map)

● **East of the town of Mammoth Lakes**

Primarily a geologic observation and interpretive site with some limited use by bathers. Open daylight hours only.

Natural mineral water emerges from many fissures as steam or boiling water and several danger areas have been fenced off for safety. Substantial amounts of boiling, geothermal water also flow up from the bottom of the creek. A bend in the creek provides a natural eddy in which the mixing of hot and cold water stays within a range of 50º to 110º. Those who venture into this confluence experience vivid thermal skin effects, but they must be careful to avoid the geothermal vents because of the danger of scalding. Bathing suits are required.

In the past, night use of this location has resulted in many injuries and some fatalities, so the area may be used only from sunrise to sunset. Citations are issued by the Forest Service to anyone found there between sunset to sunrise. During the winter, when snow blocks the access road, skiers and hikers may still enter the area during daylight hours.

Men's and women's dressing rooms are available on the premises. Overnight parking is prohibited.

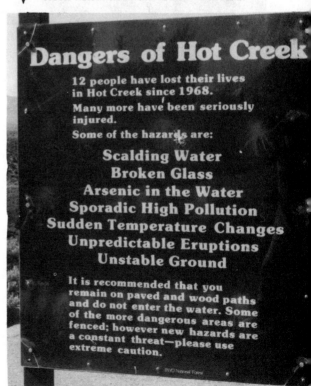

Dangers of Hot Creek

12 people have lost their lives in Hot Creek since 1968.

Many more have been seriously injured.

Some of the hazards are:

Scalding Water
Broken Glass
Arsenic in the Water
Sporadic High Pollution
Sudden Temperature Changes
Unpredictable Eruptions
Unstable Ground

It is recommended that you remain on paved and wood paths and do not enter the water. Some of the more dangerous areas are fenced; however new hazards are a constant threat—please use extreme caution.

INYO National Forest

706B   LIL' HOT CREEK

● **East of the town of Mammoth Lakes**

A very hot flowing creek fed by a 180º geothermal spring. The name *Lil' Hot Creek* has been given to a large, squishy-bottom soaking pool located just below where the flow from several cold springs cools the hot stream to approximately 107º.

Caution: Be sure to close any gates you open as you traverse the access road, and do not block the road when you park.

▲ *Shepherd Hot Spring:* According to legend, two sheep herders excavated this shallow pool just large enough for two people.

706C   SHEPHERD HOT SPRING

● **East of the town of Mammoth Lakes**

Natural mineral water flows out of a spring at 107º and through a hose to one of the first volunteer-built soaking pools in the area. The pool temperature is controlled by diverting the hot water flow when the desired soaking temperature has been reached. The apparent local custom is clothing optional.

▲ *Crab Cooker:* The volunteers who built this pool went high-tech, installing a shut-off valve in the hot water supply pipe.

► *Dave's Warm Tub:* A volunteer stone mason found the ideal place for this iron tub.

706D   CRAB COOKER

● **East of the town of Mammoth Lakes**
Natural mineral water flows out of a spring at 112º and through a pipe to a rock-and-cement soaking pool with an especially good view of the mountains. The pool temperature is controlled by turning off a valve in the pipe when the desired soaking temperature is reached. The apparent local custom is clothing optional.

706E   DAVE'S WARM TUB

● **East of the town of Mammoth Lakes**
Natural mineral water flows out of a spring at 89º and through a hose to a very private, single porcelain bathtub in a lush green ravine. The rate of flow is sufficient to maintain a temperature of 89º in the tub, so no method of temperature control is needed. The apparent local custom is clothing optional.

129 CENTRAL CALIFORNIA

Pulky's Pool: This recent high-tech volunteer effort includes valve-controlled hot and cold water supply pipes.

Crowley Hot Spring: The volunteers who built this big beauty got an assist from an earthquake which increased the outflow.

706F PULKY'S POOL

● **East of the town of Mammoth Lakes**

Natural mineral water flows out of a spring at 131º and through a pipe to a free-form, rock-and-cement pool. Of recent construction, this pool features a very smooth surface and a drain to facilitate easy cleaning. Temperature is controlled by admitting cold water piped from a nearby pond. The apparent local custom is clothing optional.

Caution: Park 100 yards south and below the nearby plateau and walk to this pool. 4WD vehicles have become stuck in the soft ground.

706G CROWLEY HOT SPRING

● **East of the town of Mammoth Lakes**

Natural mineral water flows out of a spring and down a small creek channel at 110º, then into a cement pool large enough for 30 people. Construction of such a pool was made possible by the 1983 earthquake which substantially increased the flow of geothermal water in the creek. No temperature control is necessary because surface cooling keeps the pool temperature about 103º most of the year. The apparent local custom is clothing optional.

Caution: The bog near the pool is a form of clay which remains soggy for several weeks after a heavy rain. Even 4WD's have been trapped.

706H   HOT TUB

● **East of the town of Mammoth Lakes**

Natural mineral water flows out of a spring at 110° and through a hose to a large rock-and-cement pool with a superb view of the mountains. The pool temperature is controlled by diverting the hot water inflow whenever the desired soaking temperature has been reached. The apparent local custom is clothing optional.

706I   WHITMORE HOT SPRINGS

■ P.O. Box 1609   (619) 935-4222
Mammoth Lakes, CA 93546   PR

Large, conventional public swimming pool jointly operated by Mono County and the Town of Mammoth Lakes on land leased from the Los Angeles Department of Water and Power. Open daytime; approximately mid-June to Labor Day.

Natural mineral water is pumped from a well at 90° and piped to the swimming pool where it is treated with chlorine. Depending on air temperature and wind conditions, the pool water temperature averages 82°. An adjoining shallow wading pool averages 92°. Bathing suits are required. No credit cards are accepted.

Showers, BBQ area and a full aquatic schedule are available on the premises Parking is permitted only during hours of operation.

▲ *Hot Tub:* Soakers in this low-tech pool simply push the supply hose to one side when the pool temperature is high enough.

▼ *Whitmore Hot Spring:* In the Hot Creek area this is the only site which offers tiled swimming pools and dressing rooms.

 After a long, strenuous hike a soak in one the tubs at *Red's Meadow* would feel very refreshing. No reservations necessary!

 Iva Bell: This sandy-bottom lower pool is the most convenient and the most popular at this remote location.

707 RED'S MEADOW HOT SPRINGS

● **In Red's Meadow Campground near Devil's Postpile National MonumentCRV**

Tin-roof shed with six cement shower-over bath tubs in six small private rooms, on the edge of a mountain meadow campground. Elevation 7,000 ft. Open approximately Memorial Day to September 20.

Natural mineral water flows out of the ground at 100º, into a storage tank, and then by pipe into the bathhouse. Depending on the rate of use, water temperature out of the shower heads will vary from 90 to 100º. No charge is made for the use of the tubs which are available on a first-come, first-served basis.

A Forest Service campground, open during the summer, adjoins the hot springs. It is four miles to a lodge and restaurant and 12 miles to an RV park and other services in Mammoth Lakes.

Directions: From the town of Mammoth Lakes take CA 203 west to end, then follow signs through Minaret Pass to Devil's Postpile National Monument and to Red's Meadow Campground. Note: During the day time in summer months, private vehicles are prohibited beyond Minaret Pass. A frequent shuttle bus service originates at Mammoth Mountain Inn, where there is plenty of parking, and makes many stops, including Red's Meadow Campground.

Source map: *Inyo National Forest*. USGS *Devil's Postpile*.

708 IVA BELL (FISH CREEK HOT SPRINGS)

● **South of Devil's Postpile National Monument**

A delightful cluster of volunteer-built soaking pools, some with spectacular views of the wilderness. Elevation 7,200 ft. Open all year.

This location adjoins the Iva Bell camp area which includes numerous camping sites separated by meadows and stands of pines. The two main soaking pools are not visible from the main camping area but are to be found 50 yards east, up and behind an obvious bare rock ledge.

The most popular pool has a nice sandy bottom and is nestled on the back side of this ledge where a 106º trickle flows out of a fissure slowly enough to maintain a 101º pool temperature in the summertime. A 100º squishy-bottom pool may be reached by following a path 30 yards across a meadow.

From the first pool, another path leads due east for 50 yards to a cozy campsite. From this site, a steep 100-yard path leads up to four more pools, ranging in temperature from 101º to 110º.

The twelve-mile hike (one way) from the road end at Reds Meadow involves an elevation change of 1,000 feet. Detailed directions to such a remote location are beyond the scope of this book. We recommend that you purchase *Sierra North*, published by Wilderness Press, and also consult with the Mammoth Ranger District of Inyo National Forest, P.O. Box 146, Mammoth Lakes, CA 93546. (619) 934-2505.

Source map: USGS *Devil's Postpile*.

Mono Hot Springs: This ground-level outdoor fiberglass hydropool is a recent addition to the mineral water facilities.

709A   MONO HOT SPRINGS
(Summer) Mono Hot Springs, CA 93642
(Winter) Lake Shore, CA 93634

PR+CRV+MH

709B   LITTLE EDEN

●

A vacation resort offering fishing, hiking and camping in addition to mineral baths. Located on the south fork of the San Joaquin River near Thomas Edison Lake in the Sierra National Forest. Elevation 6,500 ft. Open May to October.

Natural mineral water flows from a spring at 107º, then is piped to a bathhouse containing five two-person soaking tubs in private rooms. Customers may add cold tap water as desired to control temperature. Tubs are drained and refilled after each use, so no chemical treatment of the water is necessary. There is also an outdoor hydrojet pool which is maintained at 103-105º and is treated with chlorine. Bathing suits are required except in private rooms.

Facilities include a cafe, store, service station, cabins, campground and RV park. Massage and sweat wrap are available on the premises. Visa and MasterCard are accepted.

On the south side of the river, directly across from the resort and on National Forest land, is another hot spring supplying several old cement soaking pools, in the remains of a demolished bathhouse. Pool temperatures are approximately 101º. Bathing suits are advisable in the daytime.

Farther south are more geothermal seeps which supply warm water to a large squishy-bottom pond known as "Little Eden," maintaining a temperature of approximately 100º. From the bridge over the San Joaquin River, drive south 600 yards to a steel bridge over a penstock. Park in the turnout just beyond the steel bridge, and hike approximately 60 yards down a steep unofficial trail to the pond.

Directions to the resort: From the city of Fresno on CA 99, go 80 miles northeast on CA 168. The last 15 miles are steep, winding and rough.

These crude soaking pools are the last remnants of a bathhouse which once existed across the river from *Mono Hot Springs*.

Although a quarter mile away from the resort, this squishy-bottom Little Eden pool is considered to be part of the *Mono Hot Springs* geothermal outflow region.

Keough Hot Springs: An older historic resort, only open occasionally. Call first.

710   BLANEY HOT SPRINGS

● **Southeast of Florence Lake**

A combination hot spring and mudbath in a grassy High Sierra meadow, 9.5 miles from the road's end at Florence Lake. Elevation 7,600 feet. Open all year.

Natural mineral water oozes up through the squishy bottom of a large pool, maintaining a temperature of approximately 102º, and then flows into a nearby small, warm lake. At this remote location the apparent local custom is clothing optional.

There are no services at this location except nearby backpacker campgrounds. It is ten miles to a store, service station, etc.

The 9.5 mile trail from the road's end has an elevation gain of 1,000 feet and requires a ford across the South Fork of the San Joaquin River. It is possible to avoid 3.5 miles of that walking by riding the boat taxi, *Sierra Queen*, across the lake. Anyone hiking the part of the John Muir Trail in this region has only to hike 1.25 miles down the Florence Lake Trail to reach the springs.

Detailed directions to such a remote location are beyond the scope of this book. We recommend that you purchase a copy of *Sierra South*, published by Wilderness Press, and also consult with the Pine Ridge Ranger District, Sierra National Forest, P.O. Box 300, Shaver Lake, CA 93664. (209) 841-3311.

711A   KEOUGH HOT SPRINGS

■ Route 1, Box 9   (619) 872-1644
Bishop, CA 93514   PR+RV

Older hot springs resort in the Sierra foothills. The bathhouse is closed and swimming pool access is extremely limited. It is advisable to phone for current information. Elevation 4,200 ft. Open only when owner is feeling well.

Natural mineral water flows out of the ground at 128º and into the enclosed swimming pool (87-95º) and the wading pool (100º), using flow-through mineral water so that no chlorine needs to be added. Bathing suits are required.

Nothing is available on the premises. No credit cards are accepted. It is eight miles to the nearest restaurant, motel, service station and store.

Directions: Go seven miles south of Bishop on US 395, then follow signs west from US 395.

◆◆◆◆◆◆◆◆◆◆◆◆◆◆

Very close by is Muir Trail Ranch, which offers rustic log cabin comfort to organized groups (20 maximum) on a bring-your-own-food charter basis. Ranch guests enjoy private rock-and-tile mineral water pools.

From the road end at Florence Lake, the hiking distance is eight miles, but guests ride the ranch-owned *Sierra Queen* ferryboat for three miles across the lake and then ride ranch horses or 4-wheel-drive vehicles the remaining five miles. For information, write the owner, Adeline Smith, Box 176, Lakeshore, CA 93634 from mid-June to October, or Box 269, Ahwanee, CA 93601 in other months.

Source map: USGS *Blackcap Mountain*.

711B   KEOUGH HOT DITCH

● **Near Keough Hot Springs**

Runoff from Keough Hot Springs cools as it flows through a series of volunteer-built rock pools in a treeless foothill gully. Elevation 4,100 ft. Open all year

Natural mineral water flows out of the ground at 128º on the property of Keough Hot Springs, then wanders northeast over BLM land for about a mile before joining with a cold water surface stream. Volunteer-built rock dams create several primitive pools of various depths, each one cooler than the preceding one upstream. The apparent local custom is clothing optional.

No services are available on the premises. There is a limited amount of level, unmarked space on which overnight parking is not prohibited. It is one mile to an RV park, and eight miles to a restaurant, store and service station.

Directions: Seven miles south of Bishop on US 395, turn west on Keough Hot Springs Road approximately .6 mile. At the only intersection with a paved road (old US 395), turn north 200 yards to where a cold stream crosses the road. (Note: There is an abundance of level parking space on the north side of the cold stream, but the stream must be forded with care.) Walk an additional 50 yards north to Keough Ditch. Either stream may be followed to where they join, forming a warm swimming pond.

Keough Hot Ditch: Some of the pools are close to a parking area; plenty of other pools require no more than a short walk.

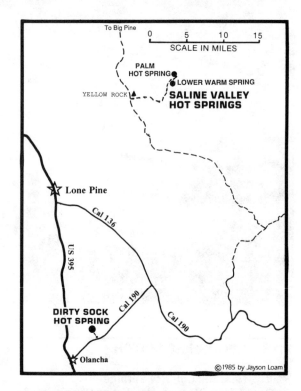

● **Northeast of the town of Olancha**

A sometimes crowded, spring-fed oasis located on a barren slope of BLM land in a remote desert valley northwest of Death Valley. Elevation 2,900 ft. Open all year, but access roads may become impassable during winter and heavy rainstorms.

Natural mineral water flows out of the two main source springs at 107º. Volunteers have installed pipes to carry this water to a variety of man-made, cement-and-rock pools for soaking, shampooing, dish washing, etc. By mutual agreement, no one bathes in the source pools. The rate of flow through the soaking pools is sufficient to eliminate the need for chemical treatment of the water. The apparent local custom in the entire area is clothing optional.

There are no services except crude volunteer-built latrines on the premises, but there is an abundance of level space on which overnight parking is not prohibited. It is more than 55 miles, half gravel surface, to a store, cafe, service station etc.

Temperatures regularly soar over the 110º mark in the summer, so this desert location with very little natural shade is preferred in the fall and spring. It becomes very crowded and should be avoided on major holidays and three-day weekends. The peace and quiet of the desert can best be enjoyed during the week.

Directions: The preferred route via Olancha is shown on the map. An alternate route starts at the north end of the town of Big Pine, on US 395. Drive northeast on CA 168 for two miles and turn right (southeast) on Death Valley Road. Drive approximately 15 miles and turn right on Waucoba-Saline Road. Drive 32 miles south to a yellow rock with a bat image on the left side of the road. Turn left (east) for six miles to the springs. Either route may be temporarily washed out by infrequent, but severe flash floods, so it is advisable to inquire about road conditions before making the trip.

Source maps: So. CA Auto Club *Death Valley.* USGS *Waucoba Wash* and *New York Butte.*

Saline Valley: Water is piped away from source pools such as this one. By mutual agreement, no one ever soaks in them.

Saline Hot Springs offers a large variety of pools at this very popular desert hot spring. The source pools are not soaked in keeping the water clean and special pools have been designated for bathing.

Volunteers at *Saline Hot Springs* have even piped running geothermal water to a special sink for washing dishes. Drain water is then piped away from the area.

▲ *Dirty Sock Hot Spring:* It is possible for adventurous people to actually take a dip in Dirty Sock, but who would want to?

▲ Whoever built this pool at *Kern Hot Spring* must have meant it for no more than three good friends.

713   DIRTY SOCK HOT SPRING

● **Near the town of Olancha**

Large, shallow pool, green with algae, in an open desert area. Elevation 3,600 ft. Open all year.

Natural mineral water flows up from the bottom of a circular, cement-edged pool at 90º and flows out at various lower temperatures, depending on wind and air temperature. The murky water gives an uninviting appearance. The apparent local custom is clothing optional.

No services are available on the premises, and there are no remaining buildings. There are many acres of unmarked level space on which overnight parking is not prohibited. It is five miles to the nearest restaurant, motel, service station and store.

Directions: From the intersection of US 395 and CA 190, go five miles northeast on CA 190. There are no signs on the highway, so look for a narrow, paved road on the northwest side and follow it 300 yards to the spring.

714   KERN HOT SPRING

● **On the upper Kern River**

A small concrete soaking pool, offering a truly spectacular view in return for a truly strenuous three-day hike from the nearest road. Elevation 6,900 ft. Open all year.

Natural water flows out of the ground at 115º directly into a shallow soaking pool built at the edge of the Kern River. Water temperature is controlled by adding buckets of cold river water as needed. Bathing suit policy is determined by the mutual consent of those present.

There are no services available except a backpacker campground 100 yards away. It is 31.5 miles west from Whitney Portal and 37 miles east from Crescent Meadow. Situated in the mile-deep canyon of the upper Kern River, this spring has a magnificent view in all directions. Detailed directions to such a remote location are beyond the scope of this book. We recommend that you purchase *Sierra South*, published by Wilderness Press, and also consult with the Tule Ranger District of the Sequoia National Forest, 32588 Highway 190, Porterville, CA 93257. (209) 539-2607.

Source map: USGS *Kern Peak*.

California Hot Springs: An old historic spa completely rebuilt for recreational family fun.

715 JORDAN HOT SPRING

● **Northwest of the town of Little Lake.**

Hot water flows meet with cold creek water on Ninemile Creek in the southernmost part of the Golden Trout Wilderness. Elevation 6,500 ft. Open all year.

Natural mineral water flows out of a spring at approximately 120º and flows down to the river where it may be mixed with cold creek water to form casual pools. Permanent pools are not permitted. The old lodge has a caretaker in the summer but there are no longer any soaking pools available.

It is six miles to the nearest road's end at the end of paved Sequoia National Forest Road 21S03, reached via County Road J41 from south of Little Lake on US 395. The trail has an elevation change of 2,500 feet. Detailed directions to such a remote location are beyond the scope of this book. We recommend that you purchase *Exploring the Southern Sierra, East Side,* published by Wilderness Press, and also consult with the Mt. Whitney Ranger District of Inyo National Forest, Lone Pine, CA 93545. (619) 876-5542.

716 CALIFORNIA HOT SPRINGS
P.O. Box 146   (805) 548-6582
■ California Hot Springs, CA 93207PR+RV

Historic resort which has been restored and expanded to offer family fun. Located in rolling foothills at the edge of Sequoia National Forest. Elevation 3,100 ft. Open all year except Thanksgiving and four days around Christmas.

Odorless natural mineral water flows out of several artesian wells at a temperature of 126º and is piped to the pool area where there are two large, tiled hydrojet spas maintained at 100º and 104º. A flow-through system eliminates the need for chemical treatment of the water. There is one large swimming pool containing filtered and chlorinated spring water which is maintained at 85º in the summer and 94º in the winter. Bathing suits are required.

The restored main building contains an office, delicatessen, ice cream parlor, pizza stand, gift shop and dressing room facilities. Massage is available on the premises. Full-hookup RV spaces are adjacent to the resort area. Visa and MasterCard are accepted. It is two miles to a motel, store and gas station.

Directions: From CA 99 between Fresno and Bakersfield, take the J22 exit at Earlimart and go east 38 miles to the resort.

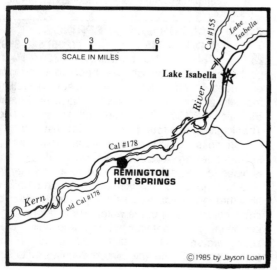

Remington Hot Springs: During high water in the Kern River this site is flooded, but the concrete pool does not wash away.

© 1985 by Jayson Loam

717 REMINGTON HOT SPRINGS
(see map)

● **Near the town of Isabella**

A delightful, two-person cement tub in an unspoiled, primitive, riverside setting of rocks and trees. Located in the Kern River Canyon down a steep trail from old Highway 178. Elevation 2,200 ft. Open all year except during high water in the river.

Natural mineral water at 104º emerges from the ground at more than 100 gallons-per-minute. This flow comes directly up through the bottom of a volunteer-built, cement tub and provides a form of hydrojet action, maintaining the pool temperature at 104º. Twenty yards uphill is a drainable, one-person rock-and-cement pool fed by a smaller flow of 96º water. Even though this site has obviously been used for many years, there is almost no unsightly trash. The apparent local custom is clothing optional.

There are no services available on the premises. It is six miles to a motel, restaurant and service station, and two miles to a Forest Service campground.

Directions: From Bodfish (by Lake Isabella) drive west on Kern Canyon Road (old CA 178, now CA 214) to Hobo Forest Service Campground. Continue west 1.5 miles to a large turn-out on the right with a telephone pole in the middle. (This is the **second** turnout with a telephone pole.) Overnight parking is not permitted. A steep, unmaintained path leads directly down to the riverbank springs, 300 yards below. Please help keep this special place beautiful by packing out all trash.

▲ *Pyramid Hot Spring:* The sandy-bottom soaking pool is under the large cube-shaped boulder mentioned in the text.
This photo was taken from the south side of the river near the parking area.

718   PYRAMID HOT SPRING

● **At the lower end of Kern River Canyon**

A delightful but hard-to-find, natural pool beneath a giant boulder at the edge of the Kern River. Open all year but not accessible during the high water of spring run-off. Elevation 1,900 ft.

Natural mineral water flows out of the ground at 109º, under a giant boulder and into a sandy-bottom soaking pool large enough for two people, where it maintains a temperature of 103º. The apparent local custom is clothing optional, but you are visible to vehicles on CA 178.

There are no services available at the location. It is one mile west to a Forest Service Campground (Live Oak) and 15 miles to all other services in Bakersfield.

Directions: From Bakersfield, go east on CA 178 to the beginning of the Kern River Canyon. Continue four miles to a marked turn-out on your left, containing a six-foot-high pyramid-shaped boulder at its east end. From the center of the turn-out, look across the river slightly eastward to locate a large cube-shaped boulder on the opposite bank. The pool is under that boulder. To reach it, follow the trail from the east end of the turn-out to the large downstream boulder where you can hop across the river. Then follow a faint unmarked path upstream to the pool. Stay low next to the river and beware of poison oak.

719   SESPE HOT SPRINGS   (see map)

● **Near the Sespe Condor Sanctuary**

A remote, undeveloped hot spring located in rugged, desert mountains subject to some flash flooding. Elevation 2,800 ft. Open all year, subject to Forest Service closures.

Natural mineral water flows out of the side of a mountain at 185º, cooling as it flows through a series of shallow, volunteer-built soaking pools. A sauna-shack steambath has also been built over the spring mouth. The apparent local custom is clothing optional.

There are no services on the premises. Access is via a nine-mile motorcycle trail from Mutau Flat, or via a 17-mile hiking trail from Lion Campground. A Forest Service permit is required to enter the area at any time. Be sure to inquire about fire-season closures, flood warnings, and the adequacy of your preparations for packing in and out.

141 CENTRAL CALIFORNIA

Big Caliente Hot Spring: According to legend, the long drive to this spring led to the invention of the redwood hot tub.

Wheeler Hot Springs: White interior paint is used in the wooden tubs to provide a smoother easier-to-clean surface.

720   WHEELER HOT SPRINGS
P.O. Box 250   (800) 227-9292
Ojai, CA 93024   PR

An historic, geothermal spa equipped with modern hot tubs in a rocky, wooded canyon in the Las Padres National Forest. Elevation 1,600 ft. Open all year.

Natural mineral water flows out of the ground at 101º and is piped to four private, indoor rooms, each equipped with a hydrojet hot tub and a cold tub. The mineral water is gas-heated to maintain a temperature of 104º on a flow-through basis, so no chemical treatment is necessary. Water from a cold spring is piped to the cold tubs on a flow-through basis so that no chemical treatment is necessary. The outdoor swimming pool, filled with chlorine-treated cold spring water and warmed by solar heat to 78º, is open all year.

Facilities include a gourmet restaurant. Construction of overnight accommodations is planned for the future; phone ahead for current status. Massage is available on the premises. Visa, MasterCard and American Express are accepted. It is seven miles to central Ojai and all other services. Phone for rates, reservations and directions.

721   THE HOURGLASS
213 W. Cota   (805) 963-1436
Santa Barbara, CA 93101   PR

Basic private-space, rent-a-tub facility located on a creekside residential street near downtown Santa Barbara.

Three private rooms with pools and eight private outdoor enclosures with pools are for rent to the public. Gas-heated tap water treated with chlorine is maintained at 104º.

A private sauna, a juice bar and massage are available on the premises. Visa and MasterCard are accepted. Phone for rates, reservations and directions.

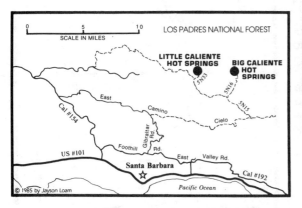

Little Caliente Hot Springs: Volunteers built and maintain both the pool and the wood sunning deck in the hills above Santa Barbara.

722A BIG CALIENTE HOT SPRINGS
(see map)

● **Near the city of Santa Barbara**

An improved, noncommercial hot spring located in a sparsely wooded canyon reached via ten miles of gravel road. Elevation 1,500 ft. Open all year, subject to fire closure.

Natural mineral water flows out of a bluff at 115º, then through a faucet-controlled pipe to a six-foot by ten-foot concrete pool. Water temperature in the pool is determined by the inflow of hot water. There is general compliance with an official NO NUDE BATHING sign.

There are government-built rest rooms and changing rooms nearby, and a year-round running stream 20 yards away. There are no other services available on the premises. A Forest Service campground is within five miles, and it is 25 miles to a restaurant, store and service station.

Source map: *Los Padres National Forest.*

722B LITTLE CALIENTE HOT SPRINGS
(see map)

● **Near the city of Santa Barbara**

A small, volunteer-built pool in a rocky canyon at the end of a wooded Forest Service road. Elevation 1,600 ft. Open all year, subject to fire-season closures.

Natural mineral water flows out of a spring at 105º and into a rock-and-cement soaking pool. An adjoining wooden sunning platform has been built by volunteers. Continual flow-through of geothermal water keeps the pool temperature constant. The apparent local custom is clothing optional.

No services are available on the premises. It is 1/4 mile to a campground and 27 miles to all other services.

Source map: *Los Padres National Forest.*

723 LAS CRUCES HOT SPRINGS

● (see map)

Near Gaviota State Park

Two primitive, mud-bottom pools on a tree-shaded slope a few miles from the ocean. Elevation 500 ft. Open all year.

Natural mineral water emerges from the ground at 96º directly into a small soaking pool and then flows into a larger pool which averages 90º. Both of these volunteer-built pools have dirt sides and cloudy water. The apparent local custom is clothing optional.

There are no services available on the premises, and overnight parking is prohibited in the parking area at the bottom of the trail. It is three miles to a campground with RV hookups and six miles to all other services.

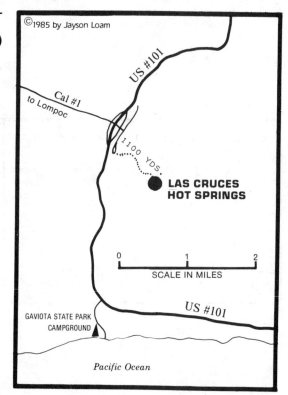

Las Cruces Hot Springs: The small pool maintains a higher temperature because it is located just below the source spring.

Avila Hot Springs Spa and RV Park: The soaking pool has an easy access ramp.

724 AVILA HOT SPRINGS SPA & RV PARK

■ **250 Avila Beach Drive** (805) 595-2359
San Luis Obispo, CA 93405 PR+CRV

Combination hot spring and RV resort located in a foothill hollow at a freeway exit. Elevation 40 ft. Open all year.

Natural mineral water flows out of an artesian well at 130º and is piped to various pools. There are six indoor, tiled Roman tubs in which the water temperature is determined by the amount of hot mineral water and cold tap water admitted. These tubs are drained and refilled after each use so that no chemical treatment is needed. The outdoor soaking pool (105º) is drained and filled daily. The 50' -by 100' outdoor swimming pool (86º) is filled with tap water treated with chlorine. Bathing suits are required except in private tub rooms.

Massage, snack bar, RV hook-ups, lawn tenting spaces and a small store are available on the premises. Visa, MasterCard, American Express and Discover are accepted. It is one mile to a motel, restaurant and service station.

Directions: From San Luis Obispo, drive south eight miles on US 101, take the Avila Beach Drive exit (not San Luis Bay Drive) and go north one block to resort entrance.

725 SYCAMORE HOT SPRINGS

1215 Avila Beach Dr.   **(805) 595-7302**
San Luis Obispo, CA 93401   **PR+MH**

Establishing an innovative new example for other hot springs to follow, this delightful resort offers dozens of secluded redwood hot tubs out under the oak trees and a private redwood hot tub on the balcony of every motel room. There are no separate men's and women's bathhouses. Located on a wooded rural hillside two miles from the ocean. Elevation 40 ft. Open all year, 24 hours per day.

Natural mineral water is pumped from a well at 110º and piped to the tubs on the hillside and on the motel balconies. Each tub has a hot mineral-water faucet and a cold tap-water faucet, so the temperature in each tub is under the control of the customer. Each tub also has its own jet pump, filter and automatic chlorinator. One of the outdoor tubs is 12 feet in diameter, capable of holding more than 40 persons. The swimming pool is filled with tap water treated with chlorine and maintained at 89º by a heat exchanger. Bathing suits are required except in motel tubs and those outdoor tubs which are screened by vines and shrubbery.

Facilities include a restaurant (Sunday brunch a specialty), motel rooms with hot tubs on the balcony (complete with Continental breakfast), a one-bedroom cottage with its own hot tub in a private enclosure, dressing rooms and a sand volleyball court. Several varieties of massage and reflexology are available on the premises. A half-hour soak in one of the outdoor tubs is included in each appointment. On request, directions to a nearby clothing-optional state beach will be given. American Express, MasterCard and Visa are accepted. Phone for rates and reservations.

Directions: From US 101 eight miles south of San Luis Obispo, take the Avila Beach exit, then go one mile west on Avila Beach Dr. and watch for resort sign on south side of road.

All of the motel units at *Sycamore Hot Springs* offer a temperature-controllable hot tub on a private-space balcony.

Esalen Institute: The unique ocean-cliff location of these pools makes it possible to hear the sea lions playing down below.

726   ESALEN INSTITUTE

Big Sur, CA 93920

(408) 667-3023
PR+MH

Primarily an educational/experiential center rather than a hot spring resort. Located on CA 1, 45 miles south of Monterey and 50 miles north of San Simeon. Elevation 100 ft. Open all year.

Esalen is a pioneer in the human potential movement, specializing in residential programs which focus on education, philosophy and the physical and behavioral sciences. Access to the grounds is by reservation only for those wishing to take workshops or come for room and board. The hot springs are also open by reservation for up to 320 people each weekday morning from 1 AM to 3:30 AM at a cost of $10 per person. To make a bath reservation please call (408) 667-3047. For a workshop or room and board information please call (408) 667-3000.

Natural mineral water flows out of the ground at 120º and into a bathhouse built on a cliff face, 50 feet above a rocky ocean beach. Within the bathhouse, which is open toward the ocean, are four concrete soaking pools and eight individual tubs. There are also two adjoining outdoor soaking pools. Water temperature is determined within each tub by admitting controlled amounts of hot mineral water and cold well water. This flow-through process, plus frequent cleaning of the pools, makes chemical treatment of the water unnecessary. Clothing is optional in and around the bathhouse.

Facilities include housing and a dining room for registered guests. Massage is available on the premises. Visa, MasterCard and American Express are accepted. It is 11 miles to a restaurant, store and service station.

727   SYKES HOT SPRING   (see map)

Near the village of Big Sur

Remote, undeveloped hot spring on the Big Sur River in the Ventana Wilderness portion of the Los Padres National Forest. Elevation 1,110 ft. May be submerged during high water in the river.

Natural mineral water flows out of the ground at 100º from under a fallen tree and into a volunteer-built shallow soaking pool. This location is a 10-mile hike on the Pine Ridge Trail and a Wilderness Permit must be obtained from the Forest Service before entering the area. However, this spring is near one of the most popular hiking routes in the wilderness, so the distance is no assurance of quiet or privacy during the summer months.

The access trail appears on USGS *Ventana Cones* and *Partington Ridge*, but the hot spring is not shown. The Forest Service issues a trail map to those holding Wilderness Permits and, on request, will mark the hot-spring location on that map.

There are no services available at the location. When you obtain your Wilderness Permit, check your preparations, including water supply, with the ranger.

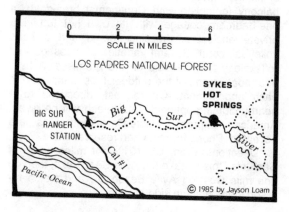

© 1985 by Jayson Loam

▲ *Paraiso Hot Springs:* The extensive grounds of this location include many palm trees, which create a tropical atmosphere.

728 TASSAJARA BUDDHIST MEDITATIONCENTER

Tassajara Springs
Overnight Reservations (415) 431-3771
Day Reservations (408) 659-2229
■ **Carmel Valley, CA 93924   PR+MH**

Primarily a Buddhist Monastery with accommodations available to the public from May 1 to Labor Day. Located in wooded mountains southeast of Monterey. Elevation 1,500 ft.

Please, no drop-in visitors. Prior reservations and confirmation required for all uses. Guests are expected to respect the spirit of a monastic community.

Natural mineral water flows out of the ground at 130º into two large, enclosed, soaking pools which average 110º. This water, which is not chemically treated, cools as it flows into nearby streambed soaking areas. The outdoor swimming pool is maintained at approximately 75º. There are also men's and women's steambaths. Bathing suits are required at swimming pool only.

Rooms and meals are included as part of confirmed overnight reservation arrangements. The use of meditation facilities is also included. No credit cards are accepted. It is 1 1/2 hours to a store, cafe and service station. The road is steep and dangerous requiring good brakes and low gears.

729 PARAISO HOT SPRINGS

                                    (408) 678-2882
■   **Soledad, CA 93960   PR+MH+CRV**

A quiet resort for adults, with several acres of tree-shaded grass areas, located on the west slopes of the Salinas Valley. Elevation 1,200 ft. Open all year.

Natural mineral water flows out of the ground at 115º and is piped to three pools; an indoor soaking pool with a temperature of 108º, an outdoor soaking pool with a temperature of 100º, and an outdoor swimming pool with a temperature of 80º. The swimming pool is treated with chlorine. Bathing suits are required. No cut-offs permitted.

Cottages, RV spaces, overnight camping and a cocktail bar are available on the premises. No credit cards are accepted. It is eight miles to a restaurant and service station.

Directions: From US 101, exit on Arroyo Seco Road, one mile south of Soledad. Go one mile west to stop sign, then go straight onto Paraiso Springs Rd. Continue uphill for six miles to resort at end of road.

147 CENTRAL CALIFORNIA

▼ *Heartwood Spa:* Massage customers arrive 15 minutes before their appointment to enjoy a soak in the outdoor communal pool.

▲ *Different Soaks:* The large hot tubs at this location provide plenty of room for families to enjoy soaking together.

730 DIFFERENT SOAKS

☐ 1157 Forest Ave.   (408) 646-8293
Pacific Grove, CA 93950   PR

Unusually spacious hot-pool rental and retail spa sales establishment located in a suburb of Monterey.

Five pools in private rooms are for rent to the public. One room has a tub large enough for ten persons, and rooms can be combined for larger groups. Gas-heated tap water treated with bromine is heated to 103º. Each room has a shower, dressing space, music speaker and a landscaped, open-roof garden along one wall.

Massage is available on the premises. No credit cards are accepted. Phone for rates, reservations and directions.

731A HEARTWOOD SPA

☐ 3150A Mission Dr.   (408) 462-2192
Santa Cruz, CA 95065   PR

A clothing-optional, tree-shaded hot tub rental establishment located on a suburban side street.

A wooden hot tub, cold tub, sauna and communal sunning areas are available for a day-rate charge. One private enclosure, with a water temperature of 105º, can be rented by the hour. All pools use gas-heated tap water treated with chlorine. Bathing suits are optional everywhere except the front desk.

Massage is available on the premises. The total facility may be chartered for private parties before and after regular business hours. No credit cards are accepted. Phone for rates, reservations and directions. (Open on Sunday evenings for women only.)

▲ *Kiva Retreat:* The sauna building, two hot pools, a cold pool, and lovely landscaping surround a central sunning lawn.

▼ *Well Within:* A Japanese garden, and tea in Japanese cups, contribute to the feeling of quiet serenity at this downtown site.

731B KIVA RETREAT

☐ 702 Water St. (408) 429-1142
Santa Cruz, CA 95060 PR

Trees, grass and flowers lend a parklike setting to this unusual, clothing-optional, hot-pool rental establishment. Located near the city center.

A single day rate gives entry to the communal grass area, two large hot tubs, a cold-tub plunge and a large sauna. Adjoining indoor dressing and social rooms are also available. Pools use gas-heated tap water and are treated with chlorine and ozone. Two private enclosures, rented by the hour, have water maintained at 102°. Bathing suits are optional everywhere except in the front entry.

Massage is available on the premises. Major credit cards are accepted. Phone for rates, reservations and directions.

731C WELL WITHIN

☐ 112 Elm St. (408) 458-9355
Santa Cruz, CA 95060 PR

Beautiful hot pool and sauna rooms overlooking a Japanese bamboo garden, located in the heart of downtown Santa Cruz.

Private-space hot pools using bromine-treated tap water are for rent to the public by the hour. There are four indoor fiberglass pools with a view of the garden. Temperatures are maintained at 104°. Two of the rooms also have saunas. Herbal tea and large towels are provided.

Massage is available on the premises. No credit cards are accepted. Phone for rates, reservations and directions.

149 CENTRAL CALIFORNIA

Lupin Naturist Club: This hydropool is at the edge of a wooded canyon, which gives the impression of being in a tree house.

732 LUPIN NATURIST CLUB
P.O. Box 1274   (408) 353-2250
☐ Los Gatos, CA 95031   PR+MH+CRV

A clothing-optional resort where both sexes are equal and the differences are accepted as natural. Located on 120 acres of tree-shaded tranquillity in the Santa Cruz mountains. Elevation 700 ft. Open all year.

Gas-heated spring water, chlorine-treated, is used in two outdoor fiberglass tubs available to all members and registered guests. Water temperature is maintained at 102-104º. Chlorine-treated well water is also used in two outdoor swimming pools, one of which is heated and covered with a plastic dome in the winter. Bathing suits are prohibited in all pools. Clothing is optional elsewhere on the grounds.

RV and camping spaces and a restaurant are available on the premises. Visa and MasterCard are accepted. It is seven miles to a motel, store and service station. Note: Future plans include building a new lodge. Phone ahead for the status of construction.

Note: This is a private club, not open to the public for drop-in visits. Phone first for information, guest passes and directions.

733 GRAND CENTRAL SAUNA AND HOT TUB CO.
376 Saratoga Ave.   (408) 247-8827
☐ San Jose, CA 95129   PR

One of a chain of urban locations established by Grand Central, the pioneer room rent-a-tub business.

Twenty one private indoor tubs are heated to 102-104º and treated with chlorine. The individual rooms each have a sauna and dressing room. Towels and soap are provided.

No credit cards or reservations are accepted. Phone for hours, rates and directions.

734 WATERCOURSE WAY
165 Channing Way   (415) 462-2000
☐ Palo Alto, CA 94301   PR

An innovative bathing center offering a variety of enjoyable rooms and experiences. The beautiful oriental decor creates a comfortable and interesting environment.

Pools, for rent to the public, use gas-heated tap water treated with chlorine and muriatic acid. Ten individually decorated private rooms each have a different combination of hot pool, cold pool, sauna and steambath. Water temperature in the pools is approximately 103º. In one of the rooms special oils or bath salts can be added to the tub as the water is drained and refilled after each use. To accommodate larger groups, two rooms can be joined.

A flotation tank for private rental, and massage are available on the premises. Visa and MasterCard are accepted. Phone for rates, reservations and directions.

735 TROPICAL GARDENS
200 San Pedro Rd.   (415) 755-8827
Colma, CA 94105   PR
Recreation-oriented rent-a-tub business sharing quarters with a racquetball facility and health club. Located a few blocks south of Daly City.

Ten private rooms with pools use gas-heated tap water treated with chlorine. Water temperature is maintained at 102-104º. A sauna is included in seven of the rooms.

Other facilities include racquetball and handball courts, a tanning studio, Nautilus conditioning, swimming pool and locker rooms. Massage is available by appointment. No credit cards are accepted. Phone for rates, reservations and directions.

736A THE HOT TUBS
2200 Van Ness Ave.   (415) 441-TUBS
San Francisco, CA 94109   PR
One of the few stress-reduction establishments offering tile tubs and decks in a chrome and glass urban environment. Located on a main street just west of downtown.

Pools in 20 private rooms are for rent to the public. Gas-heated tap water treated with chlorine is maintained at 104º. A sauna is included.

Massage and a juice bar are available on the premises. No credit cards are accepted. Phone for rates, reservations and directions.

Watercourse Way: The Japanese decor of this suburban location calls for artistic prints rather than television sets.

736B FAMILY SAUNA SHOP
2308 Clement   (415) 221-2208
San Francisco, CA 94121   PR
One of the pioneer stress-reduction centers in San Francisco. Located in the Richmond District.

Two private rooms with pools, for rent to the public, use gas-heated tap water treated with chlorine. Water temperature is 104º.

Four private saunas are available for rent. Massage and facials are available on the premises. Visa and MasterCard are accepted. Phone for rates, reservations and directions.

736C GRAND CENTRAL SAUNA AND HOT TUB CO.
15 Fell St.   (415) 431-1370
San Francisco, CA 94102   PR
The first one of a chain of urban locations established by Grand Central, a pioneer in the private room rent-a-tub business.

Pools in 26 private rooms, each with a sauna, are for rent to the public. The pools use gas-heated tap water treated with chlorine and are maintained between 102-104º.

Credit cards are not accepted. Reservations are not accepted. Phone for rates and directions.

▲ *Shibui Gardens:* The outdoor garden redwood tub experience, in an atmosphere of warm informality, is a Shibui tradition.

737 F. JOSEPH SMITH'S MASSAGE THERAPY

☐ 158 Almonte Blvd.   (415) 383-8260
Mill Valley, CA 94941   PR

A Marin healing center with two five-foot deep hot tubs nestled under redwood trees, located in a country setting.

Two private enclosures, with water temperatures of approximately 104º, and treated with chlorine can be rented by the public. One of the tubs is available for communal use during the day. A sauna is also for rent. Bathing suits are optional in tub and sauna area.

Our prayer garden is open for relaxation, sitting and meditation. Massage and advanced body therapies are available on the premises. We also offer chiropractic and acupuncture services. Massage classes and certification programs are being offered, and workshop space is available for rent. Phone for rates, reservations and directions.

738 SHIBUI GARDENS

☐ 19 Tamalpais Ave.   (415) 457-0283
San Anselmo, CA 94960   PR

An inviting blend of Marin County natural redwood hot tubs and Japanese landscaping. Located on a suburban side-street.

Three privately enclosed hot tubs using bromine-treated, gas-heated tap water are for rent by the hour. Water temperatures range from 102-105º. One communal cold pool is also available to customers at no extra charge. Bathing suits are optional inside pool and sauna spaces.

A private indoor sauna is for rent on the premises. Massage is available. Phone for rates, reservations, and directions.

739 FROGS

☐ #10B School St. Plaza   (415)453-7647
Fairfax, CA 94930   PR

One of the first rent-a-tub facilities in the San Francisco Bay area. Located in a Marin County suburb and recently renovated by new ownership.

Wood tubs for rent to the public use gas-heated tap water magnetically polarized, treated with chlorine and maintained at 105º. There are two soaking tubs in private enclosures, plus a large communal hot tub and a cold plunge. There are two saunas (the hottest in the Bay area) and a clothing-optional sundeck.

Massage is available by appointment. Visa and MasterCard are accepted. Phone for rates, reservations and directions.

740 ALBANY SAUNA AND HOT TUBS

1002 Solano Ave.   (510) 525-6262
Albany, CA 94706   PR

One of the first of a dozen rent-a-tub establishments in the Bay Area. Located a few blocks west of San Pablo Ave.

Three privately enclosed pools, for rent to the public, use gas-heated tap water, treated with chlorine. Water temperature is maintained at approximately 105º.

Four private rock-steam saunas are available for rent. Massage, juice bar, and skin care products are available on the premises. Visa and MasterCard are accepted. Phone for rates, reservations and directions.

741A GRAND CENTRAL SAUNA AND HOT TUB CO.

1915 University Ave.   (510) 843-4343
Berkeley, CA 94704   PR

One of a chain of urban locations established by Grand Central, a pioneer in the private room rent-a-tub business.

Sixteen private rooms with pools, for rent to the public, use gas-heated tap water treated with chlorine. Water temperature varies between 102-108º. A sauna is included.

A juice bar is available on the premises. No credit cards are accepted. Reservations are not accepted. Phone for rates and directions.

741B THE BERKELEY SAUNA

1947 Milvia St.   (510) 845-2341
Berkeley, CA 94704   PR

A stress-reduction establishment located a few yards north of University Avenue.

Three private rooms with gas-heated tap water pools are available for rent to the public. The bromine-treated water is maintained at temperatures from 104-106º.

Three private saunas are also for rent. Massage is available on the premises. Visa and MasterCard are accepted. Phone for rates, reservations and directions.

742A SUNSHINE SPA

1948 Contra Costa Blvd.   (510) 685-7822
Pleasant Hill, CA 94523   PR

Funky, fun-loving, rent-a-tub business located in the Pleasant Hill Plaza, 15 miles east of Oakland.

Pools using gas-heated tap water treated with bromine are for rent to the public. There are seven private rooms, each with an in-ground hot tub, sauna, shower, massage table and mural wall. Pool temperatures range from 90-102º.

Massage is available on the premises. Visa and MasterCard are accepted. Phone for rates, reservations and directions.

742B AMERICAN FAMILY HOT TUB

88 Trelany Lane   (510) 827-2299
Pleasant Hill, CA 94523   PR

Suburban rent-a-tub establishment located a few yards west of Contra Costa Blvd.

Twelve private outdoor pools are for rent by the hour. Gas-heated tap water treated with chlorine is maintained at 102-104º.

A sauna and massage are available on the premises. Visa and MasterCard are accepted. Phone for rates, reservations and directions.

743 PIEDMONT SPRINGS

3939 Piedmont   (510) 658-5697
Oakland, CA 94611   PR

Urban rent-a-tub establishment situated in downtown Oakland.

Four hot tubs, one cedar lined and one in combination with a sauna were built outdoors in private enclosures, complete with redwood decks, changing area and shower. Water temperature is maintained at 106º but can be cooled down with hoses. All tubs are chlorine treated.

Massage, herbal facials and salt scrubs are available on the premises. Phone for rates, reservations and directions.

744 GRAND CENTRAL SAUNA AND HOT TUB CO.

17389 Hesperion Blvd.   (510) 278-8827
San Lorenzo, CA 94580   PR

One of a chain of urban locations established by Grand Central, the pioneer room rent-a-tub business.

Ten private indoor tubs are heated to 102-105º and treated with chlorine. Five tubs are equipped with saunas and five have skylights in the rooms.

No credit cards or reservations are accepted. Phone for hours, rates and directions.

745 PARADISE SPA   (51) 793-7727

5168 Mowry Ave.
Fremont, CA 94538   PR

Suburban rent-a-tub and tanning center located in shopping center right off of Highway 880.

Seven private rooms come complete with tubs and showers. The water is heated to between 102-104º and is chlorine treated. Towels and radios are supplied.

Tanning booths are available on the premises. Visa and MasterCard are accepted. Phone for rates, reservations and directions.

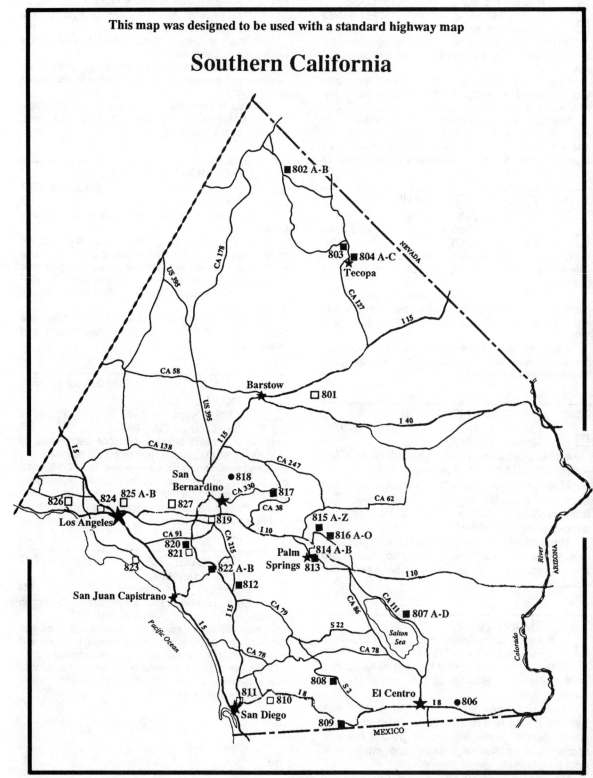

This map was designed to be used with a standard highway map

Southern California

■ 802 A-B

NEVADA

803 ■
★ 804 A-C
Tecopa

CA 178

US 395

CA 127

I 15

CA 58

US 395

Barstow
★ □ 801

I 40

I 15

CA 138

CA 247

San
Bernardino
● 818
■ 817
CA 330
CA 38

CA 62

826 □
824
825 A-B
□
□ 827
★
Los Angeles
□ 819

815 A-Z
■
■ 816 A-O

I 10

CA 91
820 ■
821 □

CA 215

Palm
Springs ★
814 A-B
813

I 10

823

822 A-B
■

■ 812

San Juan Capistrano
★

CA 79

CA 86

CA 111
■ 807 A-D

I 5

I 15

S 22

Salton
Sea

Colorado
River

ARIZONA

Pacific Ocean

CA 78

CA 78

S 2

808 ■

El Centro
★ 18 ● 806

811
★
□ 810
18

San Diego

809 ■

MEXICO

801 SILVER VALLEY SUN CLUB

☐ 48382 Silver Valley Road (619) 257-4239
Newberry Springs, CA 92365PR+MH+CRV

Southern California's first clothing-optional lake resort, located on a paved road in the high desert 26 miles east of Barstow. Sunshine 355 days per year. Elevation 1,800 ft. Open all year.

Electric-heated well water, treated with bromine, is used in an outdoor hydropool which is maintained at a temperature of 104º. Clothing is optional everywhere on the grounds, but bathing suits are prohibited in the lake, pool and showers.

Facilities include a 2.5 acre lake, air-conditioned club house, restaurant, snack bar, rental rooms, RV hookups, tent sites and exercise equipment. Volleyball, shuffleboard, horseshoes, children's games, theme parties and bingo are available on the premises. Visa and MasterCard are accepted. It is seven miles to a service station and store, 25 miles to a motel.

This is a commercial resort, affiliated with the American Sunbathing Association, open to the public. Phone for hours, rates, reservations and directions.

802A FURNACE CREEK INN RESORT

■ Box 1 (619) 786-2345
Death Valley, CA 92328 MH

An historic resort built around a lush oasis on a barren hillside overlooking Death Valley. Elevation, sea level. Open mid-October to mid-May.

Natural mineral water flows out of a spring at 89º, into two outdoor pools, and through a large, palm-shaded arroyo. The swimming pool maintains a temperature of approximately 85º, and the flow-through rate is so great that no chemical treatment of the water is necessary. Bathing suits are required. Pools are for the use of registered guests only.

Facilities include two saunas, lighted tennis courts, rooms, two restaurants, live entertainment and dancing, and a bar. Visa, MasterCard, American Express, Diners Club and Carte Blanche are accepted.

▲ *Furnace Creek Inn:* Some of the palms at this oasis date back to 20-mule team days.

802B FURNACE CREEK RANCH RESORT
Box 1   (619) 786-2345
■ Death Valley, CA 92328   PR+MH

A large, ranch-style resort in a green oasis setting. Located in the center of Death Valley, one mile west of Furnace Creek Inn. Elevation 178 ft. below sea level. Open all year.

Natural mineral water is piped from the 89º spring serving the Inn to a swimming pool at the Ranch. The rate of flow-through is so great that a temperature of approximately 85º is maintained and no chemical treatment is necessary. Pool use is open to the public as well as to registered guests. Bathing suits are required.

Facilities include rooms, three restaurants, bar, store, service station, RV hookups, golf course and lighted tennis courts. Visa, MasterCard, American Express, Diners Club and Carte Blanche are accepted.

803 SHOSHONE MOTEL AND RV PARK
Box 143   (619) 852-4335
■ Shoshone, CA 92348   PR+MH+CRV

Older resort located on CA 127 in desert foothills near the southern entrance to Death Valley. Elevation 1,600 ft. Open all year.

Natural mineral water flows out of a spring at 93º and is piped to an outdoor swimming pool. The rate of flow-through is so great that a temperature of 92º is maintained and no chemical treatment of the water is necessary. Pool use is available only to registered guests. Bathing suits are required.

Facilities include rooms, restaurant, bar, store, service station, RV hookups and overnight camping spaces. Visa, American Express and MasterCard are accepted.

Furnace Creek Ranch: Thanks to abundant geothermal flow-through, this large swimming pool needs no chlorine treatment.

Shoshone Motel and RV Park: This traditional swimming pool has no hydrojets but does have a sparkling warm waterfall.

156

804A TECOPA HOT SPRINGS RESORT
Box 420   **(619) 852-4373**
Tecopa, CA 92389   **MH+CRV**

Newer motel and RV park, located on the Tecopa loop of CA 127 in desert foothills near the Dumont sand dunes. Elevation 1,400 ft. Open all year.

Natural mineral water flows from an artesian well at 108º and is piped to seven hydropools in private rooms. Continuous flow-through maintains a temperature of approximately 107º, and no chemical treatment of the water is necessary. Posted signs require nude bathing in these pools, which are for the use of registered guests only.

Facilities include rooms, laundromat, store, RV hookups and overnight camping spaces. It is one mile to a service station. No credit cards are accepted.

804B TECOPA HIDE-A-WAY
Box 101   **(619) 852-4438**
Tecopa, CA 92389   **PR+CRV**

Small RV park located on the Tecopa loop off CA 127. Elevation 1,400 ft. Open all year.

Natural mineral water flows out of an artesian well at 118º and is piped to two indoor soaking pools where the temperature is controlled between 100-108º, depending on the season. The rate of flow-through is so great that no chemical treatment of the water is necessary. The pools are available to the public as well as to registered guests.

Facilities include RV hookups and camping spaces. No credit cards are accepted. It is one mile to a motel, restaurant, store and service station.

 Tecopa Hot Springs Resort: The hydropool building (right) overlooks the RV section of the resort and the surrounding desert.

804C TECOPA HOT SPRINGS
(operated by Inyo county)
Tecopa, CA 92389   **PR (free) +CRV**

A county-operated trailer park, bathhouse and campground located on the Tecopa loop off CA 127. Elevation 1400 ft. Open all year

Natural mineral water flows out of a spring at 108º and is piped to separate men's and women's bathhouses. Each one has two soaking pools maintained at 100º and 105º, plus an enclosed outdoor sunbathing area. Posted signs required nude bathing and also prohibit mixed bathing.

RV hookups and overnight spaces are available on the premises. No credit cards are accepted. It is two miles to a store and service station.

▲ *Highline South Hot Well*: With Interstate 8 only a few yards away, the sound level at this location varies from desert quiet to urban roar, depending on traffic volume.

806 HIGHLINE SOUTH HOT WELL

● **Near the town of Holtville**

A cement soaking pool by an artesian well, located just off the I-8 right-of-way on the east edge of Holtville. Elevation sea level. Open all year.

Natural mineral water flows out of an artesian well at 125º and splashes on the edge of a six-foot by six-foot cement cistern. Pool water temperature is controlled by diverting the hot flow after the water in the pool is as hot as desired. Because it takes so little hot water to maintain a pool temperature of more than 100º there is very little self-cleaning action and algae growth is rapid.

There are no services available on the premises and overnight parking is prohibited. However, a primitive BLM campground with a 14 day limit is located 20 yards north of the well.

Directions: At the east end of Holtville, take the Van Der Linden exit from I-8. Go north taking the first right turn onto a frontage road (Evan Hughes Hwy). Within the next few hundred yards you will cross over the Highline Canal and go past the Holdridge Road Intersection. Watch for a large parking area on your right directly opposite the BLM Hot Springs Campground sign on the north side of the road. The hot well and pool are visible at the west side of the parking area.

807A BASHFORD'S HOT MINERAL SPA
10590 Hot Mineral Spa Rd.

■ **Niland, CA 92257**   (619) 354-1315   CRV

Primarily an RV winter resort for adults, located on a desert slope overlooking the Salton Sea. Elevation 50 ft. below sea level. Open October 1 to May 30.

Natural mineral water flows out of an artesian well at 150º and into two cooling tanks from which it is piped to an outdoor swimming pool maintained at 84º and to an outdoor hydropool maintained at 102º. The water in both pools is chlorine-treated. Mineral water is also piped to six, outdoor soaking tubs with temperatures from 101-105º. These tubs are drained and refilled after each use so that no chemical treatment is needed. Bathing suits are required.

RV hookups, overnight spaces and a laundry room are available on the premises and catfish fishing (no license required) is about one mile away. Discover cards are accepted. It is seven miles to a motel, restaurant and service station.

Fountain of Youth Spa: This location is especially popular with "snowbirds", who bring their trailers south every winter.

807B FOUNTAIN OF YOUTH SPA
Rte. 1, Box 12   (619) 348-1340
Niland, CA 92257   PR+CRV

The largest and newest of the RV parks in this area, located on a desert slope overlooking the Salton Sea. Elevation, sea level. Open all year.

Natural mineral water flows out of an artesian well at 137º and into several cooling tanks, from which it is piped to two pool areas, one of which is reserved for adults. The two outdoor swimming pools range in temperature from 85-90º. The five outdoor hydropools have a variety of temperatures from 100-107º. The water in all pools is treated with chlorine. The pools are available only to registered day campers and overnight campers. Bathing suits are required.

The facilities include a laundromat, store, RV hookups, overnight camping spaces and recreation rooms. Services include massage, physical therapy, and beauty and barber shop. No credit cards accepted.

It is four miles to a motel, restaurant and service station.

807C IMPERIAL SEA VIEW HOT SPRINGS
HCO 1, Box 20   (619) 354-1204
Niland, CA 92257   CRV

The original "Old Spa" location, with the first hot well drilled in this area. Recently expanded hot-water facilities, located on a desert slope overlooking the Salton Sea. Elevation 50 ft. below sea level. Open all year.

Natural mineral water flows out of an artesian well at 165º and into a large holding and cooling tank from which it is piped to seven outdoor pools. Five hydropools are maintained at a variety of temperatures from 96-104º. One mineral-water soaking pool is maintained at 96º and an adjoining fresh-water pool is maintained at 88º. All pools are treated with chlorine. Bathing suits are required.

RV hookups, overnight camping spaces, a store and mobile home sales are available on the premises. No credit cards are accepted. It is four miles to a motel, restaurant and service station.

807D LARK SPA
Star Rte. 1, Box 10   (619) 354-1384
Niland, CA 92257   CRV

Primarily an RV winter resort for adults, located on a desert slope overlooking the Salton Sea. Elevation 50 ft. below sea level. Open all year.

Well water and mineral water, gas heated and chlorine treated, are used in an outdoor hydropool maintained at 102º. Bathing suits are required.

Overnight spaces and RV hookups are available on the premises. No credit cards are accepted. It is one mile to a store and four miles to a motel, restaurant and service station.

159 SOUTHERN CALIFORNIA

808 AGUA CALIENTE COUNTY PARK
For reservations call (619) 565-3600
PR+CRV

A county-operated, desert campground located in a wildlife refuge area near the Anza Borrego Desert. No pets are permitted at any time! Elevation 1,300 ft. Open September through May.

Natural mineral water flows out of several springs at 96º and is then piped to two pools where it is filtered and chlorinated. An outdoor pool with a water temperature usually between 80-90º is available for children. A large indoor hydropool (adults only) uses chlorine-treated mineral water and is solar-and-gas-heated to 102º. Pool facilities are available to the public for day use, as well as for those occupying campground spaces.

Facilities include RV hookups and overnight camping spaces. No credit cards are accepted. It is ten miles to a restaurant, store and gas station, and 35 miles to a motel. There is a nearby airstrip.

Agua Caliente County Park: In the indoor pool, pumps create a current around an island at a speed which provides good exercise for those who walk "upstream".

Jacumba Hot Springs: This large indoor soaking tub, with a view out to the swimming pool, makes a pleasant place to relax and talk with friends.

809 JACUMBA HOT SPRINGS HEALTH SPA
Box 466 (619) 766-4333
Jacumba, CA 92034 MH

An older motel spa located just off I-8, 80 miles east of San Diego. Elevation 2,800 ft. Open all year.

Natural mineral water flows out of a spring at 97º and is then piped to an indoor hydropool and an outdoor swimming pool. Continuous flow-through maintains a temperature of 95º in the hydropool and 85º in the swimming pool, with no chemical treatment of the water required.

Facilities include rooms, restaurant, bar and sauna, tennis and shuffle board courts. Horseback riding and guided hikes can be arranged. Massage is available on the premises. Visa, MasterCard and American Express are accepted. It is one block to a store and service station and 1/2 mile to RV hookups.

810 SWALLOWS/SUN ISLAND NUDIST RESORT

☐ 1631 Harbison Canyon Rd. (619) 445-3754
El Cajon, CA 92021 PR+MH+CRV

A large, well-equipped, traditional nudist park located in a tree-shaded canyon 15 miles east of San Diego. Elevation 500 ft. Open all year.

Gas-heated well water, chlorine treated, is used in an outdoor swimming pool with a temperature range of 75-80° and in an outdoor hydropool with water temperature maintained at 104°. Bathing suits are not permitted in pools, and clothing is prohibited everywhere, weather permitting.

Facilities include rooms, restaurant, tennis and volleyball courts, RV hookups and overnight camping. Visa and MasterCard are accepted. It is one mile to a store and eight miles to a service station.

Note: This is a membership organization not open to the public for drop-in visits, but prospective members may be issued a guest pass by prior arrangement. Resort rules prohibit guns, cameras, drugs and erotic behavior. Telephone or write for information and directions.

811 THE TUBS

☐ 7220 El Cajon Blvd. (619) 698-7727
San Diego, CA 92115 PR

San Diego's original, rent-a-tub establishment, located on a main suburban street near San Diego State University.

Eleven spa suites for rent to the public use gas-heated tap water which is treated with chlorine and maintained at 102°. Saunas are included in all rooms. The VIP Suite, large enough for 12 persons, has a bathroom and steambath in addition to a sauna.

A juice bar is available on the premises. Visa and MasterCard are accepted. Phone for rates, reservations and directions.

▲ *Murietta Hot Springs Resort and Health Spa*: Aong with massage and wonderful food, the large pool provides a wondereful place to relax.

812 MURIETTA HOT SPRINGS RESORT AND HEALTH SPA

39405 Murietta Hot Springs Rd.
(714) 677-7451
■ Murietta, CA 92362 PR+MH

A full-service resort and European health spa located two miles east of I-15 on Murietta Hot Springs Rd., 90 miles south of Los Angeles and 60 miles north of San Diego. Elevation 800 ft. Open all year.

Natural mineral water flows out of a spring at 140° and is piped to a variety of pools and tubs. The outdoor Olympic-size swimming pool is treated with chlorine and uses a combination of mineral water and cold well water to maintain a temperature of 85°. A similar combination of water is used to maintain a temperature of 102° in the outdoor Roman spa and 85° in an outdoor exercise pool. Natural mineral water is also piped to 36 indoor, one-person soaking tubs which are drained and refilled after each use so that no chemical treatment is necessary. There is a separate mud treatment section. Bathing suits are required for body wrap. Spa facilities are available to the public as well as to registered guests.

Facilities include 242 rooms, various health programs, two restaurants, beauty shop, tennis courts, a store and overnight parking. Massages, facials, herbal body glow treatments, energizing body wraps, manicures and pedicures are available on the premises. Visa, MasterCard and American Express are accepted. It is five miles to RV hookups and a service station.

Phone for rates, reservations and additional information.

Palm Springs Spa Hotel: These communal outdoor pools supplement individual tile tubs in the men's and women's bathhouses.

◀ Fresh fruit trees and beautiful flowers surround the soaking tub at *Le Petit Chateau.*

813 PALM SPRINGS SPA HOTEL

100 N. Indian Canyon Dr. (619) 325-1461
Palm Springs, CA 92262   PR+MH

A major destination resort with an elaborate mineral-water spa located in downtown Palm Springs. Elevation 500 ft. Open all year.

Natural mineral water flows out of historic Indian wells on the property at a temperature of 106º. The spa has separate men's and women's sections, each containing 14 tile tubs with mineral-water temperature separately controllable up to 104º. These tubs are drained and refilled after each use so that no chemical treatment of the water is necessary. Each spa also has vapor-inhalation rooms, a steambath and a dry sauna. Bathing suits are required in the outdoor pool area, optional in the bathhouse and solarium. Prices are discounted for hotel guests.

Services and facilities on the premises include massage, barber and beauty shop, rooms, pool bar and snacks, travel agent, airport pickup and group conference rooms. Visa, MasterCard, American Express and Diners Club are accepted. Pool and spa facilities are available to the public as well as to registered guests.

Directions: Take the Indian Ave. exit from I-10 and drive south 6 1/2 miles to the resort.

814A LE PETIT CHATEAU BED AND BREAKFAST INN

1491 Via Soledad   (619) 325-2686
Palm Springs, CA 92264   MH

Intimate, secluded hide-a-way premier clothing-optional resort located in Palm Springs' wind free south end residential area. Within easy walking distance to Indian Canyons.

Facilities include Country-French style furnished rooms(phone, TV, refrigerators, private patios), pool, spa, BBQ, and lounge in lush garden setting. Rates include breakfast and afternoon snacks. The spa is located in its own secluded garden patio and is maintained at 102º. The pool is solar heated from 85-92º. Airport pick-up service is available. Major credit cards accepted.

Phone for rates, reservations and directions.

Morningside Inn: The mural behind the pool brings a touch of the tropics to this desert resort.

Raffles Palm Springs Hotel: This central patio is small enough for a cooling misting system to work well in the summer.

814B   MORNINGSIDE INN/PARADISE DESERT RESORT

☐   888 N. Indian Canyon   (619) 325-2668
     Palm Springs, CA 92263   MH

Exclusive, secluded clothing optional resort in the heart of Palm Springs.

Fully-equipped kitchens and private patios come with each room. Gas-heated tap water is treated with chlorine and is maintained at 102° in a large hydrojet pool and 87° in the swimming pool. A misting system operates to keep customers comfortable all year around. An outdoor BBQ area is available. Airport pick-up service can be arranged. Major credit cards accepted.

Phone for rates, reservations and directions.

814C   RAFFLES PALM SPRINGS HOTEL

                        (619) 320-3949
☐   Palm Springs, CA   MH

An exotic clothing-optional oasis, named for the Singapore Raffles, in the northern part of Palm Springs. Elevation 500 ft. Open all year.

Gas-heated tap water, treated with chlorine, is used in a large hydrojet pool, which is maintained at 102º, and in a swimming pool which is maintained at 87º. Clothing is optional throughout the grounds.

Facilities and services include rooms with kitchenettes, a beautifully-landscaped central patio garden, cooled by an automatic misting system in the summer, outdoor BBQ area, and continental breakfast. Airport pick-up service is also available. Visa and MasterCard are accepted.

Phone for rates, reservations and directions.

814D   DESERT SHADOWS INN

☐   260 Chuckwalla Dr.   (619) 325-64120
     Palm Springs, CA 92262   MH

Secluded retreat for the discerning naturist with a magnificent view of the San Jacinto Mountains. Open all year.

Designer-decorated rooms come with all the amenities; kitchen suites available. Lushly landscaped grounds surround the heated pool with a covered cabana and a 24-hour courtyard hot tub. Daily breakfast buffet is included and a Saturday night bar-b-que is offered. Airport service is provided. Major credit cards accepted.

Phone for rates, reservations and directions.

All of the establishments listed below are in or near the city of Desert Hot Springs, which is ten miles north of Palm Springs. Elevation 1,200 ft. Open all year.

All of them pump natural mineral water from their own wells and offer at least one chlorine-treated swimming pool and one hydropool, where bathing suits are required.

It is one mile or less to a store, restaurant or service station. For additional information about accommodations and the general area, contact the Chamber of Commerce, P.O. Box 848, Desert Hot Springs, CA 92240. (619) 329-6403.

Directions: Take the Desert Hot Springs exit from I-10 north of Palm Springs and phone for further directions to a specific location.

Best Western Ponce De Leon Motel: Besides the central courtyard pool, this motel also has several in-room pools.

815A AMBASSADOR ARMS AND HEALTH SPA MOTEL
12921 Tamar Dr. (619) 329-1909
  (800) 569-0541
■ Desert Hot Springs, CA 92240 MH
All pools use fresh mineral water on flow-through basis. Visa and MasterCard accepted.

815B BEST WESTERN PONCE DE LEON HOTEL (in-room pools)
11000 Palm Dr. (619) 329-6484
■ Desert Hot Springs, CA 92240 PR+MH
Open to public for day-rate use. Restaurant on the premises. Visa, MasterCard, American Express, Carte Blanche, Discover and Diners Club are accepted.

815C BLUE WATER SPA
66729 Eighth St. (619) 329-6912
■ Desert Hot Springs, CA 92240 MH
Indoor hot mineral pool and jet tub. Physical therapy and massage. Major credit cards are accepted.

815D CACTUS SPRINGS LODGE
68075 Club Circle Dr. (619) 329-5776
■ Desert Hot Springs, CA 92240 MH
Visa and MasterCard are accepted.

815E CARAVAN SPA MOTEL
66810 Fourth St. (619) 329-7124
■ Desert Hot Springs, CA 92240 PR+MH
Visa and MasterCard are accepted.

815F DESERT HOT SPRINGS SPA
10805 Palm Dr. (619) 329-6495
■ Desert Hot Springs, CA 92240 PR+MH
The largest full-service spa resort in the area. The seven soaking pools and swimming pool in the central patio are open to the public for day-rate use. Facilities include a restaurant, bar and gift shop. Massage, herbal body wrap and facials are available on the premises. Visa, MasterCard, American Express, Carte Blanche and Diners Club are accepted.

▲ *Desert Hot Springs Spa:* With seven pools to choose from customers can always find a soak with just the right temperature.

815G DESERT PALMS SPA MOTEL
■ 67485 Hacienda Ave.   (619) 329-4443
  Desert Hot Springs, CA 92240   MH
Visa and MasterCard are accepted.

815H HACIENDA RIVIERA SPA
■ 67375 Hacienda Ave.   (619) 329-7010
  Desert Hot Springs, CA 92240   PR
Spa only for day use. No rooms. No credit cards are accepted.

815I KISMET LODGE
■ 13340 Mountain View   (619) 329-6451
  Desert Hot Springs, CA 92240   MH
Visa and MasterCard are accepted.

815J LAS PRIMAVERAS RESORT AND SPA
■ 66659 Sixth St.   (619) 251-1677
  Desert Hot Springs, CA 92240   MH
Visa and MasterCard are accepted.

▲ *Hacienda Riviera Spa:* The one Desert Hot Springs location offering day use only.

815K LIDO PALMS SPA MOTEL
■ 12801 Tamar Dr.   (619) 329-6033
  Desert Hot Springs, CA 92240   MH
Visa and MasterCard are accepted.

815L LINDA VISTA LODGE
67200 Hacienda Ave.   (619) 329-6401
Desert Hot Springs, CA 92240   MH
Visa and MasterCard are accepted.

815M LORANE MANOR
67751 Hacienda Ave.   (619) 329-9090
Desert Hot Springs, CA 92240   MH
No credit cards are accepted.

815N MA-HA-YAH LODGE
68111 Calle Las Tiendas (619) 329-5420
Desert Hot Springs, CA 92240   MH
No credit cards are accepted.

815O J & M MCGUIRE'S INN
13355 Palm Dr.   (619) 329-5539
Desert Hot Springs, CA 92240   MH
Visa and MasterCard are accepted.

815P MIRACLE MANOR
12589 Reposo Way   (619) 329-6641
Desert Hot Springs, CA 92240   MH
Visa and MasterCard are accepted.

815Q THE MOORS SPA MOTEL
12637 Reposo Way   (619) 329-7121
Desert Hot Springs, CA 92240
Desert Hot Springs, CA 92240 MH
Family oriented. Wheelchair accessible. No credit cards are accepted.

815R ROYAL FOX INN
14500 Palm Dr.   (619) 329-4481
Desert Hot Springs, CA 92240   MH
(in-room pools)
Restaurant on the premises. Visa, MasterCard, Discover and American Express are accepted.

815S SAHARA MOTEL
66700 E. Fifth St.   (619) 329-6666
Desert Hot Springs, CA 92240   MH
Visa and MasterCard are accepted.

815T SANDPIPER INN & SPA
12800 Foxdale Dr.   (619) 329-6455
Desert Hot Springs, CA 92240   MH
Visa and MasterCard are accepted.

815U SKYLINER SPA
12840 Inaja St.   (619) 329-3031
Desert Hot Springs, CA 92240   MH
No credit cards are accepted.

815V STARDUST MOTEL
66634 Fifth St.   (619) 329-5443
Desert Hot Springs, CA 92240   MH
Visa and MasterCard are accepted.

815W STRAW HAT LODGE
66365 Seventh St.   (619) 329-6269
Desert Hot Springs, CA 92240   MH
No credit cards are accepted.

815X SUNSET INN
67585 Hacienda Ave.   (619) 329-4488
Desert Hot Springs, CA 92240   PR+MH
Restaurant and bar on the premises. Visa, American Express and MasterCard are accepted.

815Y TRAMVIEW LODGE
11149 Sunset Ave.   (619) 329-6751
Desert Hot Springs, CA 92240   MH
No credit cards are accepted.

815Z TROPICAL MOTEL & SPA
12692 Palm Dr.   (619) 329-6610
Desert Hot Springs, CA 92240   MH
Visa and MasterCard are accepted.

Sky Valley East: Separate sets of pools for adults are available at some of the larger resorts such as this one.

All of the establishments listed below are in or near the city of Desert Hot Springs. Elevation 1,200 ft. Open all year.

All of them pump natural mineral water from their own wells and provide at least one chlorine-treated hydropool, where bathing suits are required. A store, restaurant and service station are within five miles of all locations.

Directions: Take the Desert Hot Springs exit from I-10, north of Palm Springs, and phone for further directions to a specific location.

816A AMERICAN ADVENTURE
■ 70405 Dillon Rd.   (619) 329-5371
   Desert Hot Springs, CA 92240   CRV

A family-oriented, membership recreation resort, not open to the public for drop-in visits except during the summer. Facilities include one swimming pool, three hydropools and a sauna. No credit cards are accepted.

816B CORKILL RV AND MOBILE HOME PARK
   17989 Corkill Rd.   (619) 329-5976
                              (800) 982-3714
■ Desert Hot Springs, CA 92240   CRV

Older RV park with all pools enclosed and covered. There is one swimming pool, one hydropool, one soaking pool and two cold pools. No credit cards are accepted.

816C DESERT HOT SPRINGS TRAILER PARK
   66434 W. Fifth   (619) 329-6041
■ Desert Hot Springs, CA 92240   CRV

Older trailer park within the city limits. No credit cards are accepted.

816D DESERT VIEW ADULT MOBILE PARK
   18555 Roberts Rd.   (619) 329-7079
■ Desert Hot Springs, CA 92240   CRV

Strictly a mobile home park with no RV's and no overnighters. Outdoor swimming pool and two indoor hydropools. No credit cards are accepted.

816E GOLDEN LANTERN MOBILE VILLAGE
17300 Corkill Rd.   **(619) 329-6633**
Desert Hot Springs, CA 92240   CRV

Recently renovated pool area with one outdoor swimming pool and three enclosed soaking pools. Mobile home spaces, RV hookups and overnight spaces available. New and used mobile homes are for sale. There is a restaurant, store and service station next door. No credit cards are accepted.

816F HOLMES HOT SPRINGS MOBILE PARK
69530 Dillon Rd.   **(619) 329-7934**
Desert Hot Springs, CA 92240   CRV

Older RV park with one outdoor swimming pool and one outdoor soaking pool. RV hookups and overnight spaces available. No credit cards are accepted.

816G MAGIC WATERS MOBILE HOME PARK
17551 Mt. View Rd.   **(619) 329-2600**
Desert Hot Springs, CA 92240   CRV

Well-kept, mobile home park. Hot mineral water is used in an outdoor swimming pool and an indoor hydropool. Mobile spaces, RV hookups and overnight spaces available. No credit cards are accepted.

816H MOUNTAIN VIEW MOBILE HOME PARK
15525 Mt. View Rd.   **(619) 329-5870**
Desert Hot Springs, CA 92240   CRV

Modern, mobile home park with one outdoor swimming pool and one semi-enclosed hydropool. Mobile home spaces, RV hookups and overnight spaces available. No credit cards are accepted.

816I PALM DRIVE TRAILER COURT
14881 Palm Dr.   **(619) 329-8341**
Desert hot Springs, CA 92240   CRV

Older trailer court with one soaking pool and one hydropool, open 24 hours. Mobile home spaces, RV hookups and overnight spaces available. No credit cards are accepted.

816J ROYAL FOX RV PARK
14500 Palm Dr.   **(619) 329-4481**
Desert Hot Springs, CA 92240   CRV

Large, new RV facility operated as part of the Royal Fox Inn complex. A swimming pool, two hydropools and two saunas are available to registered guests in the RV park as well as to motel guests. RV hookups are equipped with instant telephone connections through the motel switchboard.

Visa, MasterCard and American Express are accepted.

816K SAM'S FAMILY SPA
70875 Dillon Rd.   **(619) 329-6457**
Desert Hot Springs, CA 92240 PR+MH+C

One of the largest, multi-service resorts in the area with all facilities open to the public for day use as well as to registered guests. The outdoor swimming pool uses chlorinated mineral water, but the children's wading pool and four covered hydropools use flow-through mineral water which requires no chemical treatment.

Facilities include a coed sauna, motel rooms, restaurant, RV hookups, overnight spaces, store, laundromat, children's playground and gymnasium. No credit cards are accepted.

816L SKY VALLEY PARK
74565 Dillon Rd.   **(619) 329-7415**
Desert Hot Springs, CA 92240   CRV

Large, modern, landscaped mobile home and RV park. There are two outdoor swimming pools, one outdoor hydropool, two enclosed hydropools and one indoor hydropool. Facilities include men's and women's saunas, mobile home spaces, RV hookups and overnight spaces. No credit cards are accepted.

816M SKY VALLEY EAST
74711 Dillon Rd.   **(619) 329-2909**
Desert Hot Springs, CA 92240   CRV

Large, new addition to Sky Valley Park. One swimming pool, an outdoor hydropool and an enclosed hydropool are on a separate patio reserved for adults. An adjoining patio contains an outdoor swimming pool and an outdoor hydropool designed for family use.

Facilities include men's and women's saunas, mobile home spaces, RV hookups and overnight spaces. No credit cards are accepted.

816N WAGNER MOBILE HOME PARK
18801 Roberts Rd.   **(619) 329-6043**
Desert Hot Springs, CA 92240   CRV

Older mobile park with one outdoor swimming pool, two indoor hydropool and two indoor cold pools. Mobile home spaces and RV hookups are available. No overnighters. No credit cards are accepted.

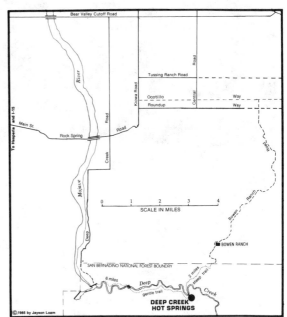

▲ The geothermal flow from other springs at *Deep Creek* is transported by pipe to provide a unique sit-down hot showerbath.

817   PAN HOT SPRINGS
420 E. North Shore Blvd.

(909) 585-2757

■   **Big Bear City, CA 92314**   **PR**

Historic indoor and outdoor swimming pools, with adjoining health club, located in the Big Bear recreation area. Elevation 6,700 ft. Open weekends in May and then every day through September 15.

Natural mineral water is pumped from a well at 90º and piped to an indoor pool which maintains a temperature of 85º. It then flows on through to the outdoor pool, which maintains a temperature of 78º. Both pools are treated with chlorine. Bathing suits are required.

Facilities include dressing rooms, health club, arcade games and a snack bar. All other services are available within five miles. No credit cards are accepted. Phone for rates, reservations and directions.

818   DEEP CREEK HOT SPRINGS
(see map)

●   **Near the town of Hesperia**

Beautiful, remote springs on the south bank of Deep Creek at the bottom of a spectacular canyon in the San Bernardino National Forest. Elevation 3,000 ft. Open all year.

Natural mineral water flows out of several rock fissures at 108º and directly into volunteer-built, rock-and-sandbag pools on the edge of Deep Creek, which flows all year. Water temperature in any one pool will depend on the amount of creek water admitted. The apparent local custom is clothing optional.

There are no services, and overnight camping is prohibited in the canyon near the springs. It is seven miles by an all-year trail to an overnight parking area. There is also a steep 2 1/2 mile trail down the north side of the canyon from Bowen Ranch, where a fee is charged for admission to the ranch and for overnight parking. From either parking area it is ten miles to a store, restaurant, service station, and all other services. Note: The trail from Bowen Ranch ends on the north bank of Deep Creek, which runs so high during spring run-off that it is not safe to try to ford the creek.

Source maps: *San Bernardino National Forest.* USGS *Lake Arrowhead.*

169 SOUTHERN CALIFORNIA

POOL RULES
1. This Pool is for Soaking Only.
2. Jumping, Diving, Splashing, Running or Horseplay is ABSOLUTELY PROHIBITED.
3. Parents are RESPONSIBLE for the BEHAVIOR & SAFETY of their CHILDREN at all times.
4. No Lifeguard on Duty at this Pool.

▲ Glen Ivy Hot Springs: A sparkling fountain sets the tone for this lovely shallow pool which was designed just for those who want to float lazily about on air mattresses.

---

819   OLIVE DELL RANCH
☐   Rte. 1, Box 393   (714) 825-6619
       Colton, CA 92324   PR+MH+CRV

A pioneer, Southern California nudist park located on a dry and sunny hilltop 60 miles east of Los Angeles. Elevation 2,000 ft. Open all year.

Gas-heated well water, chlorine treated, is used in an outdoor hydropool maintained at 105º and in a swimming pool maintained at 75º. Clothing is prohibited in the pools and in the main recreation area, optional elsewhere.

Cabins, cafe, overnight camping and RV hookups are available on the premises. It is three miles to a store and service station. Visa and MasterCard are accepted.

Note: This is a membership organization not open to the public for drop-in visits, but prospective members may be issued a guest pass by prior arrangement. Telephone or write for information and directions.

▲ Facilities at *Glen Ivy Hot Springs* include hydrojet roman-style soaking pits and larger enclosed communal soaking pools.

170

While the above pool at *Glen Ivy* is for adults only, children have a wonderful time playing in the rest of the pools, and occasionally taking a rest on a raft in this shallow floating pool.

The availability of self-applied mud treatments has earned *Glen Ivy Hot Springs* the appropriate nickname, "Club Mud".

820 GLEN IVY HOT SPRINGS
25000 Glen Ivy Road (909) 277-3529
Corona, CA 91719 PR

Large, well-equipped, beautifully landscaped day-use resort spa located on the dry east side of the Santa Ana mountains, 70 miles from Los Angeles. Elevation 1,300 ft. Open all year, except Thanksgiving and Christmas.

Natural mineral water is mixed from two wells at 90º and 110º and piped to a wide variety of pools. There are seven sunken hydrojet tubs with temperatures of 104-106º, using continuous flow-through, unchlorinated mineral water. The other pools have automatic filters and chlorinators. An outdoor swimming pool is maintained at 85º, a covered soaking pool at 103º, two outdoor hydropools at 101º and 104º, two outdoor shallow bubble pools at 103º and 100º, a large outdoor floating pool at 90º and a California red clay bath pool at 100º. (Guests should bring an old bathing suit to wear in the mud bath as the clay does stain some fabrics.) Two hydrojet pools are situated in a patio reserved for adults. Bathing suits are required.

Facilities include men's and women's locker rooms equipped with hair blowers, a coed dry sauna and two outdoor cafes. Spa treatments include Swedish, shiatsu and aromatherapy massage, eucalyptus wraps, apricot body scrubs, European facials, manicures, pedicures and waxings. Advance reservations are highly recommended. Visa and MasterCard, ATM's and personal checks are accepted.

Directions: Eight miles south of Corona on I-15, exit right onto the Temescal Canyon Rd. exit. Go one mile south to Glen Ivy Rd., turn right and go one mile to resort at end of road.

Glen Eden Sun Club: The game courts are to the right of the pools, the restaurant, showers, and rec room are to the left

822A LAKE ELSINORE HOT SPRINGS MOTEL

■ 316 N. Main   (909) 674-2581
Lake Elsinore, CA 92330   PR+MH

Older motel and spa located several blocks north of downtown Lake Elsinore. Elevation 1,300 ft. Open all year.

Natural sulphur water flows out of an artesian well at 100º and is piped to three pools and to the bathtubs in all rooms. The outdoor swimming pool is maintained at 104º. All pools are chlorine treated and are available to the public as well as to registered guests. Bathing suits are required.

Facilities include a sauna and a recreation room. Rooms and massage are available on the premises. Visa and MasterCard are accepted. It is five blocks to a restaurant, store and service station.

822B HAN'S MOTEL AND MINERAL SPA

■ 215 W. Graham   (909) 674-3551
Lake Elsinore, CA 92330   PR+MH

An older motel in downtown Lake Elsinore. Elevation 1,300 ft. Open all year.

Natural mineral water flows out of an artesian well at 120º and is piped to two pools and to the bathtubs in every room. The outdoor swimming pool is maintained at 86º, and the indoor hydropool is maintained at 105º. The water in both pools is chlorine treated and bathing suits are required.

Rooms are available on the premises. Visa and MasterCard are accepted. It is two blocks to a restaurant, store and service station.

821 GLEN EDEN SUN CLUB

□ 25999 Glen Eden Road (909) 277-4650
Corona, CA 91720   PR+CRV

Large, well-equipped, traditional nudist park located on the dry side of the Santa Ana mountains, 70 miles from Los Angeles. Elevation 1,200 ft. Open all year.

Gas-heated well water is used in an outdoor hydropool maintained at 105º and an indoor soaking pool maintained at 85º. The solar-heated swimming pool averages 75º from May to November. All pools have automatic filters and chlorinators. Bathing suits are prohibited in the pools and sauna. Nudity is expected in warm weather. Dress conforms to majority or the weather. Nights are usually cool.

Facilities include tennis and volleyball courts, sauna, restaurant, RV hookups, camping sites, rental trailers, laundry room and a recreation center. Visa and MasterCard are accepted. It is eight miles to a motel, store and service station.

Note: This is a membership organization not open to the public for drop-in visits, but prospective members may visit by prior arrangement. Telephone or write for information and directions.

 Beverly Hot Springs: This beautifully tiled pool, complete with fireplace, is in the men's bathhouse, which occupies the entire second floor of the building.

823 FAMILY HOT TUBS

2784 W. Ball Rd.　　　(714) 761-8325
Anaheim, CA 92804　　　　　　PR

Modern, suburban pool-rental facility near Disneyland and Knott's Berry Farm.

Private-space hot pools, using gas-heated tap water, are treated with chlorine. There are six indoor fiberglass pools with water temperatures maintained at 101-104º. Three of the rooms have a sauna.

Each room has a skylight, shower, hair dryer, phone, stereo system and towels. TV and VCR are available. Visa and MasterCard are accepted. Phone for rates, reservations and directions.

824 BEVERLY HOT SPRINGS

308 N. Oxford Ave.　　(213) 734-7000
Los Angeles, CA 90004　　　　PR

A modern, Korean-style, indoor spa built over a hot water artesian well a few miles west of downtown Los Angeles. Elevation 300 ft. Open all year.

From a well drilled in the early 1900's, mineral water flows out at a temperature of 105º and is piped to large, tiled soaking pools equipped with hydrojets in the women's section (first floor) and the men's section (second floor). Each section also has a pool of cooled mineral water. All pools operate on a continuous flow-through basis so that no chemical treatment of the water is necessary. Bathing suits are not required in pool rooms.

Facilities include a dry sauna and a steam sauna in each section, plus a restaurant and beauty salon. Shiatsu massage, cream massage and body scrub are available on the premises. Visa and MasterCard are accepted. Phone for rates, reservations and directions.

◀ *Family Hot Tubs:* If a big day at Disneyland gives you sore leg muscles, here is the place for your hydrotherapy.

825A-B SPLASH, THE RELAXATION SPA

☐ 10932 Santa Monica Blvd. (310) 479-4657
Los Angeles, CA 90025   PR

☐ 8054 W. 3rd St.   (213) 653-4412
Los Angeles, CA 90048   PR

Eighteen beautifully decorated, romantic, very private suites located in two urban Los Angeles locations.

All rooms feature a chlorinated hydrojet tub with controls for bubbles, water temperature, and cool-off mists. Also included are dimmer controls for room and tub lights; air conditioning; relaxation bed; fully-equipped dressing room with shower and choice of herbal soaps and towels. Many of the more exotically decorated suites offer additional amenities such as saunas, waterfalls, etc.

Gift certificates, in-suite catering, corporate memberships and overnight stays are available. Group discounts for private parties are also available, as well as help in arranging the party.

European-style therapeutic massage, aroma therapy treatment, botanical facials, body wraps, chiropractic and naturapathic care are available as well as acupuncture and homeopathic medicine. Major credit cards are accepted. Phone, for rates, reservations and directions.

Caves with romantic places to relax, and delicious picnics are just two of the many amenities available to you at either one of *Splash's* facilities. Saunas and waterfalls are a real treat in these urban locations.

 Puddingstone Hot Tubs: All tubs have a view of a large lake during the day and this panorama of city lights at night.

827 PUDDINGSTONE HOT TUBS

P.O. Box 284   (714) 592-2222
La Verne, CA 91750   PR

A unique, modern rent-a-tub facility which offers both privacy and a spectacular view. Located in Bonelli County Regional Park, overlooking Puddingstone Reservoir, 25 miles east of Los Angeles.

Fifteen outdoor pools using chlorine-treated tap water heated by a combination of propane and electricity, are for rent to the public. The very large community tub has a 360º view with spacious decking, fire pit and barbecue. The smaller tubs offer a beautiful view, tub temperature controls and a three-sided enclosure for privacy.

A wedding gazebo is available on the premises. An RV park, golf course, picnic area, horse stables, boat rentals and Raging Waters recreation area are available in the adjoining regional park. Phone for rates, reservations and directions.

826 ELYSIUM INSTITUTE

814 Robinson Rd.   (310) 455-1000
Topanga, CA 90290   PR+CRV

Tree-shaded, rolling lawns are part of a ten-acre, clothing-optional growth center located in smog-free Topanga Canyon, 30 miles west of Los Angeles. Elevation 1,000 ft. Open all year.

Gas-heated tap water, chlorine treated, is used in a large outdoor hydropool maintained at a temperature of 105º. Chlorine-treated tap water is also used in a gas-heated swimming pool. Clothing is optional everywhere on the grounds.

Massage, sauna, tennis, volleyball, recreation room and educational/experimental workshops and seminars are available on the premises. There is also a seasonal snack bar on weekends. Visa and MasterCard are accepted. It is two miles to a store, cafe and service station, and seven miles to a motel room.

Note: This is a membership organization, but nonmembers are welcome to attend all seminars and to visit. Phone or write for a copy of the Elysium *Journal of the Senses* (JOTS), and *Elysium Living Newsletter* which describes all programs.

 Elysium Institute: Some soaking in this large hydrojet pool is often included in the seminars and workshops offered here.

"Jayson didn't merely stick a toe in to test the water. He plunged in head-first and came up grinning. It is no wonder Jayson's career took off when he began publishing his guidebooks to hot springs. Hot springs symbolize Jayson Loam--bubbly warmth coming from deep inside, invigorating those along the path. Jayson has perhaps been in more hot water than any other person in the world. His guidebooks are known to hot springs lovers around the globe. To many, the name Jayson Loam and "hot springs" will remain inextricably linked."

Justine Hill, Regional Contributor, who spent many hours, over more than twenty years, talking and working with Jayson up at Elysium.

CALIFORNIA'S HISTORICAL HOT SPRINGS
Photos and text by Raymond W. Hillman

Mineral spring and hot spring resorts have been part of California's varied natural resources even long before Statehood in 1850. The original inhabitants of the region, the Native American Indians, discovered and used many of these springs - the later development of some of them surely would have astonished them.

Starting in the early 1850s Californians saw the beginnings of what would, literally, become a legion of hundreds of resorts throughout the length and breadth of their State. Two of the very oldest resorts are still welcoming guests, Vichy Springs near Ukiah in Mendocino County, and White Sulphur Springs near St. Helena in Napa County. These resorts and the hundreds that followed were a transplantation of a social and medical tradition from the Eastern United States where, for example, Poland and Saratoga Springs were famous. Still operating in the South is White Sulphur Springs in Virginia. These resorts and others continued, in turn, the European tradition of "taking the waters" in long-established spas in Belgium and Germany.

Using other United States and European counterparts for comparison, the California spas developed fame for their curative properties, invariably with the endorsement, if not the partnership, of well-known and not so well-known physicians. Collectively they established California as "one huge sanitarium." Shortly after 1900 the state was promoted as a health resort - a land where the invalid had a second and perhaps last chance to regain health. The cures were as varied as the resort facilities. The hot and cold mineral waters could cure those who were too thin with a "salt glow bath"(Agua Caliente, Sonoma County); skin problems with "arsenic beauty baths" (Seigler, Lake County); venereal diseases (Witter Spring, Lake County); stomach and urinary tract weaknesses (Bartlett Spring, Lake County, Napa Soda Spring, Napa County and many others); and those tortured with rheumatism often chose Byron Hot Springs (Contra Costa County).

The draw of Bartlett was particularly remarkable for, even today, it is not an easy journey. Once Nice on the Clear Lake north shore is reached, a dozen miles of old stage road still awaits. In the nineteenth century, before the ease of auto travel, resort guests, including those quite ill, would have to travel from San Francisco, for example, to Vallejo by steamer, train to Calistoga, ride the stage around Mt. St. Helena to the shore of Clear Lake, cross the lake by steamer, and then prepare for the final and dramatic stage run into the mountains on a winding, steep trip that took hours to the extensive Bartlett Spring resort. There was a staff of 250 to attend the guests at the five hotels, and 350 cabins.

▲ The Pagoda Spring building (burned down in 1954) at *Soda Springs* in Napa was one of the posh resorts built to resemble resorts in the East and in Europe.

This post card of the *Harbin Springs* hotel which burned down in 1960 shows a typical wood-frame verandahed hotel of a California mineral spring.

Once at Bartlettt, like most other resorts, one would usually stay for a month or so engaging in drinking or bathing in the waters and also playing croquet, bowling, attending concerts, or simply engaging in games and conversation with a circle of friends on extensive verandahs. Those who could not afford to venture to the California spas could still benefit from the waters as dozens of spas and bottling works provided extensive distribution of the drinking water to distant parts of the United States.

The resorts were traditions in every sense. Richardson Springs near Chico was operated by three generations of the same family; Hobergs (Lake Co.) was managed from 1918-1970 by George Hoberg, who was born, lived and died at the resort. Napa Soda Springs was developed for thirty years to a nineteenth century elegance beyond all others by Col. John Jackson. He was so dedicated to the spa that when asked if he would sell the resort he responded, "Do you want me to sell my soul, sir? My heart is tied up in these springs."

Today, much of the tradition is gone, the stone buildings of Napa Soda have become one of California's more exquisite ruins. With the "automobile age" rapidly changing life styles, many former guests wanted to have the freedom of moving about in their motor car and not spend all their vacation time at one resort. The development of attractions at Lake Tahoe and highway improvement in the Sierra Nevada drew thousands in another direction. The old resorts declined and started to close. Richardson Springs, Harbin, Seigler springs and many others have become religious retreats or acquired religious sponsorship. Some, like Indian Springs in Calistoga, survived without closing. Others, like White Sulphur, Wilbur and Vichy, have rebounded from decades of neglect to greet guests once again. This is largely due to the resurgence of interest in mineral water that has swept Californians within the last twenty years to, happily, reestablish California as a large health resort.

Raymond W. Hillman, professional historian and narrator of "Historic Springs and Spas" tours can be reached at (800) 400-1849.

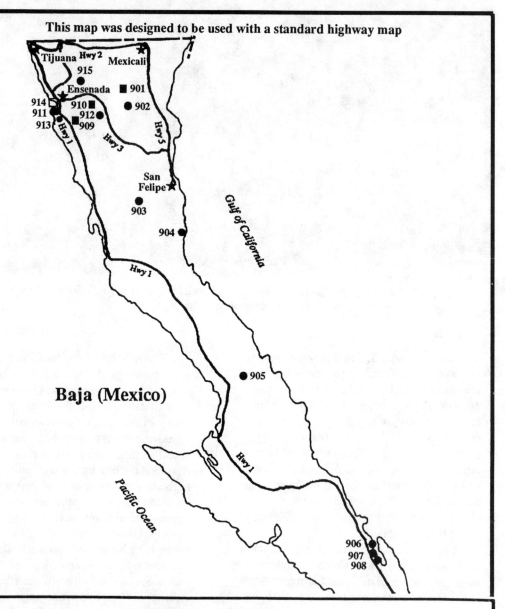

This map was designed to be used with a standard highway map

Tijuana Hwy 2 Mexicali

915

■ 901

Ensenada

914 910 ■ 902

911 912 ●

913 909

Hwy 1 Hwy 3 Hwy 5

San Felipe

903

904

Gulf of California

Hwy 1

905

Baja (Mexico)

Hwy 1

Pacific Ocean

906
907
908

MAP AND DIRECTORY SYMBOLS

● Non-commercial mineral water pool   ～～～ Paved highway

■ Commercial (fee) mineral water pool   - - - - Unpaved road

□ Gas-heated tap or well water pool   ····· Hiking route

PR = Tubs or pools for rent by hour, day or treatment

MH = Rooms, cabins or dormitory spaces for rent by day, week or month

CRV = Camping or vehicle parking spaces, some with hookups,
       for rent by day, week, month or year

One of the sparkling pools to be found at *Guadalupe Canyon Hot Springs* offering magnificent desert vistas.

901 GUADALUPE CANYON HOT SPRINGS

A young boy, a cave area to explore, and a soak -an unbeatable combination at *Guadalupe Canyon.*

■ **Southwest of Mexicali   PR+CRV**

Beautiful mineral water soaking pools, waterfalls and campsites in a remote palm canyon on the east slope of the Sierra Juarez Mountains. Elevation 1,300 ft. Open all year, but summer temperatures often reach 110º.

Natural mineral water emerges from several springs at 125º and flows through man-made aqueducts to pools, showers and flush toilets. More than twenty drainable soaking pools, built of rocks and cement, are scattered through palm forests and piles of boulders. Bathing suits are required except at night.

A limited number of campsites at Campo #1, each with its own parking area, pool and picnic table, can be rented by the day, week or month. This Campo has new restrooms and some newer tubs.Contact Rob's Baja Tours, P.O. Box 4003, Balboa, CA 92661. (714) 673-2670. For reservations, Campo #1. The other camps are owned by the Loya brothers (Rob's brothers-in-law).

There is no electricity or telephone at this location. All services are 60 miles away in Mexicali, but there is a small store which sells cold beer and soft drinks. Ancient Indian caves, cascading waterfalls and thick palm forests are within hiking distance. Other palm canyons in the mountain range may be explored for primitive hot springs but the use of an experienced guide is recommended (Rob's Baja Tours).

Directions: Drive west from Mexicali on Hwy 2 to marker K28. Turn south onto a graded dirt road for 27 miles to an intersection bordered by large alfalfa fields. Turn right onto a sandy road which winds up into Guadalupe Canyon.

This is one of several cold-water pools and waterfalls supplied by an all-year stream running through *Guadalupe Canyon*.

A rentable campsite at *Guadalupe Canyon* includes a shaded picnic table and a fire pit in addition to its own soaking pool.

After a day exploring *Guadalupe Canyon* there is nothing quite like watching the sunset from a relaxing hot pool.

▲ *Valle Chico Hot Springs:* In such remote locations there are few volunteer-built pools because there are few volunteers.

◀ *Palomar Canyon Hot Springs:* This is another remote site which needs some inspired pool-building volunteers.

902   PALOMAR CANYON HOT SPRINGS

● **Southwest of Mexicali**

Small wilderness hot springs in a remote palm canyon on the east slope of the Sierra Juarez Mountains, 45 miles from the nearest paved road. Elevation 1,500 ft. Open all year, but summer temperatures often reach 110º.

Natural mineral water bubbles out of three small source pools at 98º and then sinks into the sand as it flows down the canyon. No soaking pools have yet been built. At this remote location the apparent local clothing custom is the mutual consent of those present.

There are no facilities or services, but there is an all-year cold water stream in the canyon and excellent camping locations for backpackers. Four wheel drive is required on the last few miles of the access road, and the springs are a two hour hike up the canyon beyond the end of the road.

Directions to such a remote location are beyond the scope of this book. The use of a guide service such as Rob's Baja Tours is recommended.

903   VALLE CHICO HOT SPRINGS

● **Southwest of San Felipe**

A remote primitive hot spring in a barren canyon in the eastern escarpment of the Sierra San Pedro Martir. Elevation 1,500 ft. Open all year, but summer temperatures often exceed 110º.

Natural mineral water bubbles out of a large source pool at 144º and flows across the canyon into an all-year cold water stream. Volunteers could build a soaking pool at that confluence but have not yet done so. At this remote location the apparent clothing custom is the mutual consent of those present.

There are no services at this location. Directions to such a remote location are beyond the scope of this book. The use of a guide service such a Rob's Baja Tours is recommended.

Puertecitos Hot Springs: Bring a tide table to determine when to soak here.

---

904 PUERTECITOS HOT SPRINGS
● **On the Gulf of California**
South of San Felipe

Shallow geothermal pools accumulated in volcanic rock fissures which are underwater during high tide. Elevation sea level. Open all year.

Natural mineral water flows up through the gravel bottom of numerous gulf-edge fissures. Pool temperatures vary widely, depending on the mix of geothermal water and sea water. Bathing suits are recommended.

There are no services at this location. It is 1/4 mile to all services in the town of Puertecitos.

Directions: From San Felipe, follow Hwy 5 for 52 miles south to the town of Puertecitos. When you reach the Pemex station on your left, turn left and follow that street for 1/4 mile to where it ends in a cul-de-sac. Return 75 yards back toward Hwy 5 and look on the gulf side of the street for a cement path through volcanic rock down to the soaking pools.

---

905 MISSION SAN BORJA

●
East of the town of Rosarito

A small historic source pool on the grounds of a well-preserved mission in a remote and enchanting part of the Sierra La Libertad. Elevation 2,200 ft. Open all year.

Natural mineral water at 96° flows out of a rock-lined source pool built by the missionaries in the early 1800's. It is located at the edge of the mission cornfields, a five minute walk southeast from the main building. The runoff from the spring was commingled with a nearby cold stream to water the mission's fields. Bathing suits are required.

There are no facilities or services, but camping is permitted anywhere among the ruins of old mission buildings.

Directions: At Rosarito, on Hwy 1, turn east on a dirt road for 21 miles. There will be no sign for the mission, but there are two ranchos on the way, and the road ends in a remote valley containing the mission.

Mission San Borja: This source pool was lined with rocks nearly 200 years ago

▲ *Santispac Beach:* This is the volunteer-built soaking pool which is usable all of the time because it is located above the level reached by high tide waters.

906   SANTISPAC BEACH
●   **Concepcion Bay**
         South of Mulege   CRV

Two squishy-bottom soaking pools built by volunteers near a mangrove swamp on the edge of the Bay. Elevation - sea level. Open all year.

Natural mineral water oozes up through the rock-encircled mud bottom of one source spring, maintaining a temperature of 106º, except when flooded by high tide. A second source spring, on slightly higher ground, has been excavated by volunteers to create a squishy-bottom pool which maintains a temperature of 102º. Bathing suits are required.

Santispac beach is a popular RV and camping destination on the Sea of Cortez. Camping is $5 per car per night and there is a small restaurant on the beach. All other services are ten miles north in Mulege.

Directions: From Mulege, drive ten miles south on Hwy 1 and turn left into the commercial parking/camping ground. Drive to the far right side of the cove, to a small area for parking, and walk approximately 100 yards on a dirt trail around the mangrove swamp to the two pools.

▲ One of the attractions of *Santispac Beach* is the commercial campground located right on the edge of the Sea of Cortez.

Concepcion Beach: This is another location where you need to bring a tide table to determine when there will be enough sea water to cool down the geothermal water.

907   CONCEPCION BEACH
● **Concepcion Bay**
  South of Mulege

On the edge of a beautiful bay, very hot water flows from rock fissures into rock-and-sand pools which are soakable only when the high tide brings cold water for mixing. Elevation - sea level. Open all year.

Natural mineral water flows out of cracks above the high tide line at more than 135º into volunteer-built soaking pools on the beach below. Twice a day the high tide supplies enough cold water to bring the pool temperatures down to tolerable soaking levels. Bathing suits are required.

Directions: There are no direct routes down the steep cliffs which border this beach, Therefore, it is necessary to hike south along the tide pools from Santispac Beach (see #705 above) or north from Los Cocos Beach.

908   EL COYOTE WARM SPRING
●   **Concepcion Bay**
    South of Mulege   **CRV**

A small permanent soaking pool in a fantastic setting on the edge of Concepcion Bay. Elevation - sea level. Open all year.

Natural mineral water seeps into a tide pool at the base of a cliff. Volunteers have built a rock-and-concrete wall around the tide pool, which maintains a temperature of 86° at low tide. Small shrimp have been observed in the warm partly-salty water. Bathing suits are required.

The camping fee at El Coyote Beach is $10 per night, but there is no additional fee for using the hot spring. There are no other facilities at the beach but there is a restaurant at Rancho El Coyote across the highway. All other services are 17 miles away in Mulege.

Directions: From Mulege, drive 17 miles south on Hwy 1 to the El Coyote Beach commercial campground. Park and follow a rocky trail 100 yards to the pool.

 El Coyote Warm Springs: The absence of cold sea water enables this pool to get up to its maximum temperature of 86 degrees.

909   URUAPAN HOT SPRINGS

■   **South of Ensenada**   **PR**

A well-worn combination bathhouse and laundry in a green fertile valley at the base of coastal scrub foothills two miles from Hwy 1. Elevation 500 ft. Open all year.

Natural mineral water flows out of many pastureland springs at temperatures ranging from 118° to 138° and is piped to a cistern which supplies a 50-year-old building with five individual bathtub rooms and five outdoor washing machines. Clearly, the tubs are for cleanliness bathing, not recreational soaking, and clothing is optional only in the private-space bathtub rooms.

There are no services available, but overnight camping is permitted. It is two miles to a comfortable campground at Hwy 1, and ten miles to all other services in Ensenada.

Directions: From Ensenada, drive south on Hwy 1 to marker KM 42. Turn left (east) at Uruapan sign on dirt road, drive 2 miles through the village of Uruapan and watch for "Banos Thermales" signs. The hard-pack dirt road is in fair condition until it crosses a river, and may be impassable in winter.

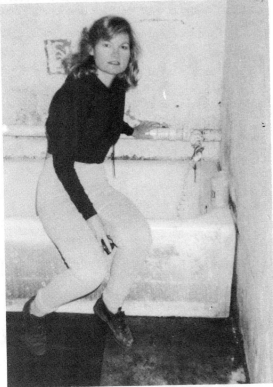

Uruapan Hot Springs: These are one-person tubs rented for the sole purpose of bathing, not for group recreation.

Agua Caliente Hot Springs: The bathhouse building and motel units are on the far side of the slide-equipped soaking pool.

910   AGUA CALIENTE HOT SPRINGS
PR+MH

■   **East of Ensenada**

An older commercial hot springs "resort" located in a arid valley five miles south of Hwy 3. Elevation 1,500 ft. Open all year, but the bar and restaurant are open only during April, May, June, July and August. Natural mineral water flows out of several springs at temperatures ranging from 80 to 108º. The warmest source spring supplies 108º water to the bathhouse tubs which are drained and filled after each use.. It also flows directly into a large concrete outdoor soaking pool where it maintains a temperature of 97º. Water from the coolest spring is piped to a large swimming pool which is drained and filled every week, resulting in a temperature of 75°. No chemical treatment is added to the mineral water. Water from a third spring (97º) is piped to the motel rooms, bar and restaurant as tap water. Bathing suits are required except in private-space individual tubs.

Motel rooms are available on the premises, with bar and restaurant service during spring and summer months only. It is 16 miles to all other services in Ensenada.

Directions: (Do not attempt in wet weather) From Ensenada, drive east on Hwy 3 to marker KM26. Watch for AGUA CALIENTE sign and turn right on a five-mile dirt road which ends at the resort. It is not recommended for trailers or low clearance vehicles.

Since this location does not have a telephone or mailing address it is not possible to secure reservations. The location is usually very crowded during Easter vacation.

911   PUNTA BANDA HOT SPRINGS
●   **Estero Beach**
On the Punta Banda Peninsula

A unique opportunity to literally dig-your-own hot spring pool at low tide on an easily accessible beach south of Ensenada. Elevation sea level. Open all year.

Natural mineral water (up to 170º) bubbles up through many yards of beach sand. During high tide swimmers can feel the extra warmth in the surf. During low tide it is possible to dig pools in the beach sand which fill with a soakable combination of hot mineral water and cold sea water. Bathing suits are required.

RV spaces are available in the adjoining trailer camp which offers its tenants hot mineral water piped from geothermal wells on the premises. It is eight miles to all other services in Ensenada.

Directions: From Ensenada, drive south on Hwy 1 to Hwy 23 Maneadero. Turn right on the paved road for approximately eight miles to the Agua Caliente Trailer Camp. This beach is also known as La Jolla and is near the Baja Beach and Tennis Club.

Punta Banda Hot Springs: Bring a shovel to dig your own volunteer-built geothermal pool at low tide, but expect it to be destroyed during the next high tide.

 Valle Trinidad offers the choice of soaking in sandy-bottomed, brick-lined pools or out in the middle of the stream.

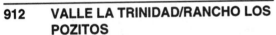

912 VALLE LA TRINIDAD/RANCHO LOS POZITOS
Near Valle Trinidad
Southeast of Ensenada

Sandy bottom pools, semi-developed, at the head waters of a stream in an open valley. Surrounded by small hills, low mountains, and agricultural lands in the midst of old rancheros. Elevation 2,800 ft. Open all year.

Natural mineral water flows up from the bottom of the first pool at 105°. This eight-foot square pool has a sandy bottom, brick walls and tin roof. The second pool is lined with rocks and located in the middle of the stream. In the third pool water flows into a six-foot square brick pool. Bathing suits are required.

Overnight parking is permitted at the farm house, about 100 yards away. It is five mile to a store, restaurant and other services.

Directions: Go east out of Ensenada on Highway 3 about 60 miles. Turn right toward Valle Trinidad on paved road. Go one mile and turn right onto dirt road at church. Continue two miles toward west end of valley and follow dirt road about five miles with some signs for San Isidoro. Look for Rancho Los Pozitos, Familia Arballo.

913 RANCHO GILBERTO
● **Near Santo Tomas**
South of Ensenada

Hot water comes up in several locations in a small stream which flows down into a valley surrounded by farming areas and treed hillsides. Elevation 500 ft. Open all year.

Natural mineral water flows up from under the stream at 100º in several places. You will need to dig your own pool and place rocks and sand around the edge to hold the water. Temperatures are regulated by mixing hot water with cold stream water. Bathing suits are required.

There are no services on the premises but overnight parking is available at the farm house, 100 yards away. It is 15 miles to a campground at La Bocana Beach and four mile to a store and restaurant.

Directions: From Ensenada travel 20 mils south on Highway 1. Turn right on dirt road with sign for La Bocana. Drive 4.1 miles on graded dirt road towards ocean. Rancho on left side, no sign.

 Walking in the streams at *Rancho Gilberto* you can feel the hot water flowing up and build yourself a pool to soak in.

The hydrojet pool at *Las Rosas Hotel & Spa* is beautifully tiled and provides guests with a similar view of the shoreline.

914 LAS ROSAS HOTEL & SPA
Post Office Box 316   PR+MH
Ensenada, Baja California, Mexico
□   Telephone: (706) 674-4310

A charming small hotel/resort on the magnificent shoreline north of Ensenada. Elevation sea level. Open all year.

Tap water, heated with kerosene, is used in a seaside pool maintained at 80º and in a hydrojet spa maintained at 104º. Bathing suits are required. Pools are available for day use except during busiest summer months. Inquire by telephone to determine current status.

Rooms, restaurant, fitness center and racquetball court are available on the premises. It is two miles to all other services in Ensenada. Visa and MasterCard are accepted.

Directions: From Tijuana, take the Hwy 1 toll road south for 60 miles to Las Rosas, which is two miles north of Ensenada.

Russian Valley Hot Springs: Only 1/4 mile from the arid surroundings of this pool there is a cold stream and waterfall.

915 RUSSIAN VALLEY HOT SPRINGS

● **South of Tecate**

Several undeveloped wilderness hot springs near a beautiful waterfall in a remote valley which was named for an historic Russian settlement. Elevation 1,500 feet. Open all year.

Natural mineral water flows from two main source springs at 125º. In one sandy-bottom pool the geothermal water bubbles up from below and is cooled by evaporation to maintain the pool temperature at approximately 110º. The other source spring flows out of a sandy bank into a rock-lined pool where it is mixed with creek water, and the temperature is controlled by moving rocks to admit more or less cold water. In this remote location the apparent local clothing custom in the mutual consent of those present.

There are no services on the premises, but there is a delightful cold pool and waterfall beside the access trail a quarter mile from the springs. All services are 25 miles away in Ensenada.

The hot springs area is located 50 miles south of Tecate and ten miles east of Hwy 3. Detailed directions to such a remote location are beyond the scope of this book. We recommend the use of a guide service such as Rob's Baja Tours.

Those who are soaking in one of the Russian Valley Hot Springs seldom worry about city traffic noise or pollution.

The **American Sunbathing Association** is a 50-year old national nudist organization which is the US representative in the International Naturist Federation. The A.S.A. annually published a Nudist Park Guide, containing complete information about nudism in all of the local parks and clubs. The A.S.A. also publishes informational pamphlets which are free for the asking. Send your inquiry to:

American Sunbathing Association
1703 North Main St.
Kissimmee, FL 32743

The **Naturist Society**, which started as a free beach movement, has expanded its goals to include legalization of nude swimming and sunbathing on designated public land, including parks and forests as well as beaches. It offers individual membership and publishes a quarterly journal about clothing optional opportunities. If you would like to know more, address your inquiry to:

The Naturist Society
PO Box 132
Oshkosh, WI 54902

The *Hot Springs Gazette* was the pioneering hot-springs periodical created seventeen years ago as an irreverent and irregular quarterly by Eric Irving. It featured personal accounts of hot spring adventures sent in by subscribers and hot spring enthusiasts. David Bybee will be taking the publication in some new directions in the future. Subscriptions, single copies and back issues are available. Send inquiries to Dave at:

Hot Spring Odysseys
5322 Centinela Ave.
Los Angeles, CA 90066-6908

AQUA THERMAL ACCESS is the publisher of *Hot Springs and Hot Pools of the Northwest* and *of the Southwest*, the most complete and accurate guide books on the subject. We need your help to maintain that level of quality. If you discover a situation which requires a change, an addition or a deletion, please send the information to:

ATA Publishing
55 Azalea Lane
Santa Cruz, CA 95060

It is always sad to report that another natural hot springs has gone NUBP (Not Useable by the Public). This time it was a favorite in Southern California known as OH MY GOD HOT WELL. The authorities, rather than coming up with a cooperative solution, came in and dynamited the well and filled it in with concrete.

Alphabetical Master Index

This index is designed to help you locate a listing when you start with the location name. The description of the location will be found on the page number given for that name.

Within the index the abbreviations listed below are used to identify the specific state or geographical area of the location. The number shown after each state listed below is the page number where the KEY MAP of that state will be found.

AZ = Arizona / 88
BJ = Baja (Mexico) / 178
CCA = Central California / 118
CO = Colorado / 42
NV = Nevada / 22
NM = New Mexico / 70
NCA = Northern California / 100
SCA = Southern California / 154
TX = Texas / 66
UT = Utah / 34
NUBP = Not Usable By the Public

If you discover that the description of a location needs to be revised, jot the information down here and then send it to:

ATA Directory Editor
55 Azalea Lane
Santa Cruz, CA 95060

BOOK MAIL ORDER

Name _____

Street _____

City _____ State ____ Zip ____

Each book: $14.95 + $2.00 shipping = $16.95	Order Quan.	Amount
Hot Springs and Hot Pools of the Northwest $16.95		
Hot Springs and Hot Pools of the Southwest $16.95		
Day Trips in Nature: CALIFORNIA $16.95		
		TOTAL

Make check to: AQUA THERMAL ACCESS

Mail to: 55 Azalea Lane, Santa Cruz, CA 95060

Canadian Buyers:
Send payment in US dollars or add $3 to Canadian funds.

BOOK MAIL ORDER

Name _____

Street _____

City _____ State ____ Zip ____

Each book: $14.95 + $2.00 shipping = $16.95	Order Quan.	Amount
Hot Springs and Hot Pools of the Northwest $16.95		
Hot Springs and Hot Pools of the Southwest $16.95		
Day Trips in Nature: CALIFORNIA $16.95		
		TOTAL

Make check to: AQUA THERMAL ACCESS

Mail to: 55 Azalea Lane, Santa Cruz, CA 95060

Canadian Buyers:
Send payment in US dollars or add $3 to Canadian funds.

Name				
Street				
City		State	Zip	
Each book: $14.95 + $2.00 shipping = $16.95			Order Quan.	Amount
Hot Springs and Hot Pools of the Northwest			$16.95	
Hot Springs and Hot Pools of the Southwest			$16.95	
Day Trips in Nature: CALIFORNIA			$16.95	
Make check to: AQUA THERMAL ACCESS				TOTAL
Mail to: 55 Azalea Lane, Santa Cruz, CA 95060				

**BOOK
MAIL ORDER**

Canadian Buyers:
Send payment in US
dollars or add $3 to
Canadian funds.

Name				
Street				
City		State	Zip	
Each book: $14.95 + $2.00 shipping = $16.95			Order Quan.	Amount
Hot Springs and Hot Pools of the Northwest			$16.95	
Hot Springs and Hot Pools of the Southwest			$16.95	
Day Trips in Nature: CALIFORNIA			$16.95	
Make check to: AQUA THERMAL ACCESS				TOTAL
Mail to: 55 Azalea Lane, Santa Cruz, CA 95060				

**BOOK
MAIL ORDER**